PENGU ON THE ROCKS

SURVIVING THE RAF REGIMENT – AN AIRMAN'S STORY

BY

BOB 'TAFF' PRICE

First published 2016 by Compass-Publishing
www.compass-publishing.com

ISBN: 978-1-907308-82-6

A catalogue copy of this book is available from the British
Library.

Typeset, printed and bound by Book Printing UK
Remus House, Coltsfoot Drive
Woodston, Peterborough PE2 9BF
www.bookprintinguk.com

DEDICATION

This book is dedicated to Number 1 Squadron Royal Air Force Regiment and in particular to those who served on the squadron when it was based at RAAF Butterworth, Malaya during the time of the Indonesian Confrontation.

PREVIOUS BOOKS BY THE AUTHOR

UFOs Over Hampshire and the Isle of Wight. Ensign Publications Southampton 1990. Updated and re-released by Halsgrove Publications 1996.

Life on the Airliners. Brooks Books Southampton 1991.

Men of the Year. Brooks Books Southampton 1991.

The Explicit Guide to Coarse Running. Canopy Books Southampton 2001.

Wheels Up. Woodfield Publishing 2003.

ACKNOWLEDGEMENTS

I received a lot of help from a lot of people when writing this book and my sincere thanks go to all who gave of their time willingly and cheerfully. To George Gault, who runs the RAF Regiment Website (RAF Regiment 1964 – 1970) who did so much to start the ball rolling when he put me in touch with past members of 1 LAA during the time I served with them, a big thank you.

To John Harris, who I shamelessly bombarded with emails requesting information and whose very good book, *'Pull up a Sandbag and Pass me a Lamp,'* proved an excellent source of material for my own book. To Ron Taylor, who shared with me some 'interesting' times in mid-air with the Penang Services Parachute Club and also for the wonderful cartoon. Ian Nisbett, who went to the trouble of sending me loads of photographs from the time and helped me out with some of the more remote areas of my memory!

To Brian Gale, who heard the East a-calling and now lives in the land he once defended, thanks for filling in some of the blanks.

Nick 'Streaky' Bacon in Canada for a very detailed account of life on the squadron, not to mention his role in 'encouraging' me out of a Huey helicopter in Malaya! All the boys on our ex Boy Entrant talk group, 'Hereford Bullocks,' for putting up with years of jungle and airborne 'heroism' stories with good humour and great fortitude! Now they've got them all in a book as well! Special thanks to the group moderator, Mickie Collins, for his invaluable help with the illustrations and some complicated computer stuff!

Finally, to every one of those hard nosed, good natured rock apes who proved such good comrades on 1 LAA during my time with the squadron. This book is for all of you.

Bob 'Taff' Price

FOREWORD

Penguin on the Rocks is a book that offers a different look at life on a Royal Air Force Regiment squadron. It's written by a man whose trade in the RAF was Supply/Air Movements but who found himself seconded to 1 LAA (Light Anti Aircraft) Squadron as part of their two man stores team. It could be said that it was a self inflicted posting as you will find out at the beginning of the book but, far from bemoaning his luck at being stuck with a bunch of 'rock apes' he threw himself into regiment life with immense gusto. Knowing personally of his enthusiasm whilst serving with us in Malaya it led me to saying of him on my RAF Regiment website that, at times, Taff was more of a 'rock' than most 'rocks!' He's been afforded the title of Honorary Rock Ape, something he values highly and his book clearly reflects the affection he held (and still holds) for the RAF Regiment.

This book is an excellent look at the lives of young men serving overseas, often in difficult and demanding circumstances and it pulls no punches with its often colourful language. This is as it should be. Rock apes were known for many things by many people but moderation of language wasn't one of them! *Penguin on the Rocks* is both exciting and informative. It's a very good read for anyone. Even penguins…!

George Gault (Gunner)
1 LAA Squadron RAF Regiment, Malaya 1966

INTRODUCTION

To read this book without a quick look at service life in the sixties would result in knowing only part of the story. Tours of duty in Malaya at that time were lengthy, two and a half year tours and single men could expect to say goodbye to their families and friends in the sure and certain knowledge that they wouldn't be seeing them again for the whole of that period. There would be no home leave granted unless an immediate relative died.

We had no mobile telephones and no computers or laptops. We couldn't even make a telephone call home without enormous expense and even then only after making a booking for a time and date. There was also the problem that some of our parents didn't have telephones anyway. Mine certainly didn't. Our only means of communicating was by hand written letter and these took four days to reach the recipient. Add a day or two for the reply to be sent and you'd be looking at a letter every ten days or so. Add to that the reluctance with which many seemed to approach the task of writing letters home and you could expect to be out of touch for anything up to three weeks. Often longer, if you were away on exercise.

There was no air conditioning in our billets and no television. If you were lucky there'd be a television room somewhere on camp but most of the programmes out there were in the Malay language, which didn't help us much at all. We knew we'd be spending two Christmases out there and, if you were fortunate, one of the married families would welcome you into their homes for a home cooked dinner. It was a bit of a tradition and very welcome. One I was lucky enough to enjoy, courtesy of one of my regiment mates and his wife. If you were unlucky you'd be stuck on duty and miss everything. My second Christmas Day in Malaya was spent in the cab of a three tonner, stuck in Butterworth Ferry Port. Our Christmas dinner came courtesy of a nearby bar. A large bottle of Tiger beer apiece and a couple of cigarettes, both enjoyed in the cab because we weren't allowed to leave the truck unattended.

There was also a rather unusual affliction that got to quite a few of us out in the Far East. I thought it was something that only affected me but I soon found out I wasn't alone. After about two years I began to think I'd never been anywhere else but the Far East! We spent our entire tour out there; even when we were on leave and it's safe to assume that a lot of us had a hard time adjusting when we came back home. 1 LAA didn't have that problem when they were posted home though. Before they had time to adjust they were sent to Cyprus on UN peacekeeping duties.

Health and safety, likewise, wasn't a term we were familiar with at the time and some of the situations we were put in would nowadays have packs of lawyers circling for a no win, no fee compensation claim. We didn't have unions to fight our cause and if we fell off a ladder or maybe even a chair there'd be no claim for duty of care failure against the management. A concise, "Clumsy bastard," was all we got for our pains and maybe even a deduction of pay if we broke whatever we fell off!

In other words, it was a very different world to the one we live in today. We were different men to the ones we are today as well and I'd like to assure my son and daughter that the dad they know now is nothing like the person in this book. Hopefully, I left him behind in Malaya when I came home!

I hope this book will be read with enjoyment. I've written it in a fairly light hearted manner because joking and cynical, coarse humour helped us cope with a life that could have been unbearable otherwise. I also hope that it will bring a little more understanding of the RAF Regiment and what it's like to serve with them.

Bob (Taff) Price

A BRIEF EXPLANATION

PENGUINS: Anybody in the RAF who isn't in the RAF Regiment.

ROCK APES: Everybody in the RAF Regiment.

Why call them Rock Apes? Opinions differ as to the exact incident that prompted the nickname but it's generally understood that it came about when two RAF Regiment officers serving in Dhala (a state in the British Aden Protectorate) decided to venture forth and shoot a few Hamadryas Baboons. The Baboons were known locally as rock apes.

Unfortunately they decided to split up and, in the half light one of them took a shot at what he thought was a rock ape moving ahead of him. It turned out to be his brother officer who was apparently less than pleased! Luckily, the wounded officer survived and was fit to resume duties a few months later.

The Board of Inquiry naturally wanted to know why the offending officer shot his comrade. He replied that, in the poor light, his comrade looked just like a rock ape! This story quickly went on the 'Grapevine' and the RAF Regiment became known for ever more as 'rock apes,' or 'rocks' for the shorter version.

Another story has it that, during World War 2, the Germans picked up on the legend that if the Barbary Apes of

Gibraltar ever left, the British Empire would crumble. For propaganda purposes they planned a raid to wipe out the apes. The story has it that Winston Churchill came to hear about this mission and tasked the RAF Regiment with protecting the apes, thereby creating the nickname. There is another version but the origin is vague and probably best left that way. It clearly didn't come from anyone who was a fan of the RAF Regiment because it was short and brutally to the point.

"Because they have the mental capacity of a rock and act like apes!"

THE MOTTO ON THE SQUADRON CREST IS WRITTEN IN ANCIENT ASSYRIAN.

IT TRANSLATES AS 'ARKISH, SURRISH' MEANING 'SWIFTLY AND SUDDENLY.'

Number 1 Light Anti Aircraft Squadron Royal Air Force Regiment Malaya 1966

CHAPTER 1

A TOUCH OF THE SUN

"Taff, get in here, son. I've got good news and bad news for you!"

Well, that's just bloody great then isn't it? Why does there always have to be an element of bad news with everything in the Royal Air Force? I'd just walked into the Air Movements hangar at RAF Lyneham after a bitterly cold stint loading a Britannia aircraft with freight. I was wearing all the cold weather clothing I could get my hands on and looked like a labourer from a North Sea oil rig!

Responding to the call from my section sergeant I went into his office and luxuriated in the warm glow of the two electric fires he had as a perk to rank. Our crew room had one ancient stove that gave off very little heat but chucked out volumes of asphyxiating smoke to compensate.

"Hello, Sarge," I said warily, "What's the news then?"

"The good news is that you can get rid of all that cold weather gear for a start," he grinned, "The bad news is that you can go and draw out tropical kit because you're posted."

I was just nineteen years old at the time but I'd been in the RAF since the age of fifteen when I joined as a boy entrant. All I'd ever wanted since leaving boys service was an overseas posting and now I'd got my wish but was it about to turn sour on me. At the time (1965) nearly everybody I knew who went abroad was sent to bloody Aden and that was the last place on earth I wanted to go. I'd been there on a flight from Lyneham and spent just two days there before flying back again. It was enough for me to decide that if I ever got posted to Aden I'd desert and join the Royal Navy!

"Where to, Sarge?" I asked, pulse moving up a couple of gears.

"Butterworth," he replied with a huge smile on his face, as though he'd just told me I'd won the pools or something.

"Oh, Ye-essss!" I exulted, "Not bloody Aden. Great. Thanks very much Sarge - where's Butterworth anyway?"

"Christ almighty," he breathed "It's in Malaya you ignorant sod. On the mainland just across from Penang Island. It's a RAAF (Royal Australian Air Force) base with a small RAF Element attached. "

A few short months later I was boarding a British Eagle Airways Britannia in London for the long, almost 10,000 mile haul to Singapore where I'd be starting out on what I considered to be a great adventure. I was still nineteen, single and looking forward to almost three years of adventure and excitement in the jungles of Malaya. Such are the dreams of youth and, as with most dreams, they tend to come crashing down around your ears with a resounding clatter...

CHAPTER 2

BEWARE WHAT YOU WISH FOR

When we landed at Singapore the servicemen among us were taken to the transit billet to await transport to our respective destinations. There were just three of us for Butterworth and this meant another flight up country to get there. This one was a tiny bit different from the civilian airliner we'd arrived in though.

BRISTOL 'FRIGHTENER'

"Gentlemen, in the likely event of a crash please follow these instructions…!"

So went the welcoming words of a crew member stood in the doorway of a Bristol Freighter aircraft of the Royal New Zealand Air Force. We came to know this aeroplane as a Bristol 'Frightener' during our time out there. It was horrendously noisy and vibrated so badly it's a miracle it didn't fall apart. There was no heating, no air con and no pretty stewardesses to cater for our every need. We had a journey of almost 370 miles in this aeroplane, quite a lot of it over hostile jungle and it's safe to say that when we touched down at Butterworth there were at least three of us who'd sworn everlasting allegiance to our Lord if he got us down safely!

I fully expected to be posted to an air movements section as I'd just finished a year at Lyneham in this role. To enlighten you briefly I'd passed out of boys service as a supplier (stores) but volunteered for one of the first air movements courses about six months later. It was much to my liking and I thought and hoped that I'd be on air movements for the rest of my time in the RAF. There you go again. Optimism - the curse of teenagers. When I touched down at Butterworth I was still only nineteen years of age and looking forward to an exciting time in the jungles of Malaya!

"Welcome to Butterworth, Price. You'll be reporting to stores tomorrow morning. You'll like it there. It's nice and quiet."

And quiet it was. Dreadfully, mind numbingly quiet. They put me in a small office with two very pretty Eurasian girls but I was blinded to their charms sad to say. I spent at least a month in there doing a very boring job and the thought of being in there for two and a half years almost put me on the 'At risk of self harm' list!

I applied for a move and met up with the flight lieutenant in charge of my section. He was unmoved by my pleas to get out to something a bit more exciting and told me to just get on with it. We had regular meetings of this nature. Now this is where I deviate from the factual to the guesswork. We had Squadron Leader Arnold (Jeff) in charge of our stores and I firmly believe to this day that it was down to him that I went on to enjoy my tour of duty. I can only guess that they would have had regular meetings between officers and NCOs to discuss any problems within the section and I think my name must have popped up on several occasions as an ingrate who didn't realise when he was well off. Whatever the reason I was moved out of that office and put in charge of Forward Supply.

Forward Supply was a great little job. There was only me and a civilian driver on the strength. Our job was to load up a van with all the spares required by the various squadrons and units on the base and shove off to deliver them. It was a lovely job with plenty of freedom and I was happy for at least six months. Then I began to fret that this still wasn't what I was expecting from a tour of duty in Malaya. Where were all the jungle patrols with rifles at the ready? Why were we not in jungle green instead of the boring KD (Khaki Drill) uniforms we were all lumbered with? I didn't expect to be fighting bandits in close quarter combat nor, to be honest, did I want to. I did expect a bit of jungle experience though and a chance to make up a few stories of terrible hardships to impress everyone back home. It didn't happen though did it? I knew a lot of store men (or suppliers as they preferred to be called) who spent the whole two and a half years of their tour in the same office without even getting a sniff of jungle.

"Look son, what exactly are you looking for out here? What did you expect to find?" These words came from my chief tech (my boss) who was once again listening to me going on about the lack of excitement in my life.

"I expected a bit of adventure, Chief," I told him, "this is Malaya after all and so far I haven't seen any jungle other than from the inside of a bloody aeroplane."

He looked at me long and hard before grunting, "Hmmmm..." and wandering off.

Not long afterwards I was summoned in to see the chief. I thought I was in for a bollocking but not this time.

"Ah, Taff," he beamed, which worried me somewhat because he only called me Taff when there was bad news to be broken.

"We're taking you off forward supply and sending you to the RAF Regiment. Report to 1 LAA (Light Anti Aircraft) Squadron on Monday," he announced. Well, not to put too fine a point on it, I was stunned. I'd only come across the RAF Regiment twice before and both experiences weren't what I'd call happy ones. In boys service our drill instructor was a regiment corporal and he was one of the hardest men I ever came across. He ran us ragged for eighteen long months. He was asked once what the RAF Regiment was exactly and he just said, "It's the army, son."

The second time I came into contact with them is covered in a later chapter. Now I was off to join a whole squadron of them!

"Beware of what you wish for, young man," beamed the chief, "Now bugger off."

CHAPTER 3

GUNS AND GREENS

When I reported to 1 squadron stores I was met by Sergeant Shorter. This was our full complement. Me and him! One sergeant and one senior aircraftman. Our stores' building wasn't all that big and most of it was taken up with racks of equipment and sealed ration packs.

"First things first," I was told, "Get over to clothing stores and get yourself a set of jungle greens, jungle boots and full webbing. Then go to the armoury and sort out your personal weapon which, God help us all, will be a Stirling Sub Machine Gun."

Oh Ye-ssss! Jungle greens and a machine gun. My face must have lit up because dear old Sergeant Shorter looked pained and told me to sod off and get myself kitted out. I needed no second bidding.

At the armoury I was issued with my SMG (number 41) and shown how to clean it. Lots of oil involved naturally and I came away smelling like a locomotive engineer! All I wanted now was a chance to shoot something! Anything really, provided it wasn't shooting back. I got my chance on the firing range but it was a bit of a let-down. The SMG looked suitably menacing but, in truth, if you were stood more than five feet away from your target the chances of hitting it were remote. Well, it was for me anyway.

I was taken around the various sections to be introduced to my new colleagues and the CO; Squadron Leader Adams asked me if I knew anything about 1 LAA. I was forced to admit that I didn't. He pointed out a framed scroll on the wall and told me to spend a few minutes reading it. It was a potted history of the squadron and I learned that it had originally been formed in 1921 as Number 1 Armoured Car Company. It had a distinguished record of action in Iraq, Kurdistan, Egypt and Palestine. In 1941 it formed part of the beleaguered RAF Station at Habbaniya which successfully fought off a force of over 9000 troops of the rebellious Iraqi Army. It was incorporated into the RAF Regiment in 1946. The Squadron was re-roled on a number of occasions to a field Squadron, internal Security unit and a light anti aircraft squadron. When I was attached to them it was in the role of a light anti aircraft squadron and was equipped with 40/70 Bofors guns. Along with 111 Battery Royal Australian Artillery they were chiefly responsible for airfield defence. 1 LAA had three manned positions. The North ORP, South ORP and the beach gun. ORP standing for 'Of Runway Position.'

It didn't take me long to get settled in and as I came to know the regiment boys I was delighted to find out that they weren't anywhere near as bad as they were painted by the rest of the RAF. Not all of them anyway! I soon got used to them tramping about the place in boots and Puttees and enjoyed all the banter we exchanged. For the first time since arriving in the Far East I felt as though I'd maybe found what I was looking for. I desperately hoped I wasn't going to be disappointed again and that I might just find that little bit of adventure I was yearning for.

CHAPTER 4

LOOK AT ALL THAT GREEN STUFF

"Have you ever been up in a helicopter, Price,"

"No, sir."

"Have you ever been in the jungle?"

"No, sir."

"Okay, get your gear together then. We'll be off in an hour for a bit of jungle experience."

Oh, Ye-esssssss!

There were two experienced regiment officers, one brand new pilot officer and little old me in the group. The idea was to give us jungle virgins a taste of the ULU (jungle) in all its glory. I frantically changed into my jungle greens, filled my water bottle, stuck a machete on my belt and slung my SMG over my shoulder. As I approached the waiting officers, I was greeted with the words,

"Christ almighty, where d'you think you're going? We'll be gone five or six hours maximum. We're not going trekking up the bloody Amazon!"

Well, I didn't know did I but I was allowed to keep it all anyway. They could see how disappointed I'd have been if I'd had to leave it all behind.

"Look son, when we want an air strike called in or some poor bastard shot we'll let you know but for now just ditch the commando outfit and hand that bloody rifle back, okay?"

A Whirlwind helicopter took us to our destination which was a small clearing in the jungle. It couldn't land because it was a bit soggy underfoot as it were but it hovered low enough for us to jump out without breaking anything. We made our way to firmer ground while the Whirlwind set off back to camp. The idea was to navigate our way through the jungle and return to our drop off point for the flight back. If we failed to get back in time the helicopter would return to camp and we'd make for an alternative RV point where, hopefully, a three tonner would be waiting for us.

WHIRLWIND HELICOPTER

As we entered the jungle I got my first taste of its eerie presence. It was all enveloping and a little bit menacing if truth be told. It didn't help that my over hyped imagination had snakes slithering behind every bush and scorpions under every stone! The heat was stifling and every sound had my eyes swivelling like windscreen wipers. I didn't see a single animal all the time we were there. I was hugely disappointed!

The officer class had a bash at navigating with the compass and then made the mistake of handing it to me.

"See if you can get us back to the RV point without getting lost," said the Boss. Well, I tried, I really did but we ended up in almost impenetrable undergrowth anyway. I even got to use my machete which was great fun. I ended up drenched in sweat and entangled in what felt like half the Malayan jungle.

"SO THIS IS THE MALAYAN JUNGLE – IT'S VERY GREEN ISN'T IT?"

"Okay, good effort," I was told, "Now give me that bloody compass back."
Bit rude I thought but didn't pursue the point. The upshot was that we only just made it back to the RV point in time. Nobody blamed me exactly but I could feel this sort of tense atmosphere whenever they glanced in my direction. Things didn't get any better when the helicopter arrived either.

A couple of aborted attempts were made to clamber aboard the Whirlwind as it hovered over the clearing until, eventually, the pilot signalled that he'd have to winch us up. The Boss went first to show us how to do it but once he was on board the pilot decided to make one more effort to get low enough for the rest of us to scramble aboard. This time we managed but it was hard work and I was left like a landed fish on the floor of the helicopter, gasping for what little air there was. Then, and this I found a little disconcerting, the pilot couldn't generate enough lift to get us out of the clearing. He tried crabbing sideways to one end and then 'taking a run' back across to gain a bit more speed. He tried, without success, a couple of times and then came the dread news.

"I'm going to try once more but if it still doesn't work, two of you'll have to get off and we'll pick you up in the morning. By the time we get back to Butterworth it'll be too dark to come back for you."

I tried to crawl into a small space at the back of the cabin so as not to be noticed but the Boss grinned across at me and said, "Well, you're the one carrying enough weight to sink a bloody battleship!"

Mercifully, on the third run we sort of staggered into the air and climbed slowly over the treetops. I offered a prayer of thanksgiving for the skill of RAF helicopter pilots and enjoyed the rest of the journey back to base.

It was the sort of adventure I'd craved for when I came out to the Far East. I hoped it wasn't to be the last. Happily for me, the RAF Regiment ensured it wasn't.

CHAPTER 5

GETTING TO KNOW YOU

I'd been on the squadron for a couple of months when Sergeant Shorter left for a home posting and was replaced by Sergeant 'Jock' Mercer. Jock was a smashing bloke and we worked well together. He'd served with a regiment squadron before and knew what he was about. It was thanks to Jock that I was able to take part in so many activities with the squadron. Providing I covered some of his weekends to allow him to play cricket he was happy enough to let me off the leash when required. He reckoned he saved my life once...

"What're you doing this weekend, Taff?" he asked me on one occasion. In fact I was due to make my first free fall parachute descent but Jock just told me he was playing cricket and I was going to be on duty whatever I was supposed to be doing. I'll never forget his parting words.

"Good lad," he said, "I've probably saved your fucking life anyway...!"

Bless his tartan socks. I hoped he'd be out for a duck!

I was beginning to find out about regiment humour as well. It was a bit on the rough side sometimes. On one occasion I was at the back of the stores when Gunner Bill Twist walked in. He had a hand grenade in his hands and was looking a bit puzzled.

"Taff, have a look at this for me mate and let me know if it's safe." With this he threw the grenade at me. With a terrifying PING! The hand lever flew off in mid air. Now, I didn't know a lot about hand grenades. We didn't have much call for them in stores nor even on Air Movements but I'd seen enough war films to know that the pin being pulled and the lever flying off preceded a big bang. I was almost out of the door before Bill started laughing and told me it was only a dud used for practice! It took me a long time to regain my colour and composure. I wanted to hurt him really but he was a big lad so I let it go. Humour wasn't just left to the gunners though and the squadron warrant officer, Frank Sylvester had his own unique brand of cruel humour.

Frank was a gruff voiced Grimsby man with years of service behind him and had scant regard for anyone's finer feelings. When one particular gunner found himself on a charge for some misdemeanour or other (Not sure what the offence was – probably fighting or being drunk!) he was stood alongside Frank, whose job it was to lead him inside to stand before the

CO and face a verdict. His chances of being found innocent and sent on his way were shattered when Frank opened the door to the CO's office and called out, "Shall I march the guilty bastard in now, sir?"

I wasn't immune to his ministrations either. We had a squadron gathering on Penang one riotous night. It was a real hoot and that's about as much as I remember. When I woke up in the morning I was in jail! The camp guardroom to be exact, minus belt and shoe laces to avoid the risk of hanging myself and generating a lot of paperwork and bother for the MPs on duty. I had no idea why I was there but when I got up and went over to hold on to the cell bars to steady myself I found myself looking at Scouse in the opposite cell. He looked as bad as I felt.

"What the fuck're you doing in here, Taff," he croaked.

"No idea, Scouse. What about you?"

"Haven't got a fucking clue!" he admitted.

One of the squadron officers came up to get us out and it was all rather humiliating. I went back to the billet to get changed and then tried to sneak into my little stores haven without being seen. I had been though. Seen that is. Frank Sylvester was leaning out of his office as I crept past and immediately broke into a very loud rendition of, 'Gaoler Bring me Water,

Gaoler Bring Me Water....' This of course brought every other bugger out and I was subjected to the usual barrage of coarse humour. To make matters infinitely worse, when my charge came up I had to go before Squadron Leader Arnold, my stores commanding officer for the offence to be heard. He was a very good officer it has to be said but he had little tolerance for drink related offences and bad behaviour. I can't remember exactly what I was charged with but it was along the lines of, 'Drunk and unruly.' I came out of his office feeling about two feet high.

I blamed the company I was keeping!

CHAPTER 6

GUNS, SNAKES AND SCORPIONS

"You're off on Exercise Golf Hotel," I was told one sunny day. That's what I liked about the regiment. None of this, "Would you like to go…," or, "If it's convenient." You were off on Exercise Golf Hotel whether you liked it or not sunbeam.

Our destination was further north towards the Thai border (which is a round about way of saying I can't remember the name of the place). Basically it was a firing range set in a clearing surrounded by jungle. This, I hasten to add, wasn't for the 40/70 Bofors guns the squadron was equipped with. We'd be firing the SLR (rifle), the Bren Gun and the penguins among us would also get a bit of practice on our SMGs. The firing point had about eight pits in a line along it and these would form part of the shooting sequence. The First few rounds would be from the prone position, the next few from the kneeling position and the last would be from the standing position inside the pits. They were about five feet deep which allowed us to rest our elbows and rifle on the lip.

The clearing was hemmed in on three sides by the jungle and would have been a nice quiet spot when there weren't lots of people shooting guns off all over the place. On the first day of shooting I was stood behind my pit ready to move forward and lay down beside it for the prone shooting. I looked down the line and saw the rest of the lads in a similar position. As we moved forward closer to the pits I heard someone shout out, *"THERE'S A FUCKING SNAKE IN MY PIT!"*
Naturally, and don't ask me why it was natural because looking back on it there was an element of lunacy about it, the rest of us crowded up to have a look. As I came up to peer down into the pit this very large snake came slithering out and over the top at a terrifying speed. It went through us all like a dose of salts and scattered us all over the place. I've got two main phobias in my life and one of them happens to be snakes so this wasn't a good start for me. It seems that during the night these pits made good sleeping accommodation for snakes and we'd disturbed one of them enjoying a lie in! It wasn't pleased. I wasn't pleased and by the looks on the faces of the other lads they weren't pleased either. It was eventually killed by one of the gunners who snatched a pace stick from a hesitant pilot officer and clouted it behind the head. I suppose, looking back, this was a bit on the cruel side but the thought of it coming back for another kip soon got rid of any feelings of guilt. When all the

excitement had died down we reformed in front of our pits but it wasn't in an eager way you understand. Every one of us crept up to the pits with rifles pointed down looking for other visitors. Mine, thankfully, was clear but there were snakes in two other pits. Any thoughts of dispatching them with a bullet though, were soon discouraged.

"Don't even bloody think about firing those rifles or you'll be in a lot more trouble than if you'd got bitten in the arse by a fucking Cobra!"

Well, thank you very much indeed for your concern. Please don't fret about chucking us in a snake pit...

I enjoyed it tremendously of course, even though I disgraced myself with my SMG. The first time I took it up to the firing point one of our corporals, Jack, gave me a bit of personal instruction. I was shooting at a target that resembled a charging enemy soldier and my instructions were as follows.

"Give the bastard a burst in the guts, Taff!"

It was great fun firing off that SMG but when the target was examined there wasn't a mark on it.

"Let's try that once more," my tense instructor told me.

Well, I gave it another go and missed again. Not my fault. Bloody gun had no accuracy whatsoever. My seething corporal got up close and personal and asked me quietly if I knew how to fire a rifle.

"Yes, of course I can, Jack," I told him.

"Well, go and fucking get one," he said snatching the SMG off me, "because you're no fucking use at all with one of these are you"

Honestly, *some* people…

It was a lively sort of camp and we had some rare evenings in the mess tent it has to be said. We were under canvas and my camp bed was set up in my stores tent. It was very cramped but after a skinful of Tiger beer I felt no discomfort at all. Until I found a scorpion under my camp bed that is. The camp was infested with scorpions, mostly little brown things that didn't cause too much concern but this thing was big and black and looked lethal. It did to me anyway. Naturally, once again, my shout of dismay brought a large contingent of nosey buggers to find out what was causing alarm to their favourite penguin. The next bit isn't really very nice but the alternative was to let this thing wander around the camp and nobody really wanted this because it looked evilly dangerous. It was booted outside the tent and one of the lads suggested we put a ring of fire around it to see if it would really sting itself to death as the old myth had it. Lighter fuel was poured in a circle around the scorpion and set alight. We all looked on in morbid curiosity but all the scorpion did was stay right in the middle of this ring of fire and not move an inch. When the fire eventually went out the scorpion was drowned in a mess tin filled with fuel from one of the Tilley lamps in my tent. I actually took it back to Butterworth and went up to Sick Quarters to ask if I could have some surgical spirit to keep it preserved in. They obliged and I kept it in an empty Brylcreem jar. It was a fine specimen that I intended to bring back home with me. I didn't get the chance because it was stolen a few months later. Just as well really because I'm not sure customs would have been all that thrilled with it!

NOT REALLY CUDDLY. MALAYSIAN SCORPION

The only other bit of excitement that came my way during the exercise happened in the Butts. I was doing my bit with the target (another charging enemy soldier that had to be lifted up by means of a wooden post attached to it). I'd done this a few times and was getting a bit tired when I thought I'd just sit on one of the steps that led up from the bottom of the butts area to the target point. There were about five steps in all. When it came to me raising the target again I must have been higher than I thought because the next thing I knew there was a chunk of dirt and grass being thrown up by a poorly aimed bullet that continued on its way and took a chunk out of the target post I was holding. I think I may have flinched a bit. In fact I may have flinched a lot because the next thing I get is a bollocking for not holding the target steady . Not one word of concern for my well being nor any signs of sympathy for my plight did I get. I was getting used to the ways of the RAF Regiment by now though and none of this really surprised me!

CHAPTER 7

A FEW MINOR INCIDENTS

Between the departure of Sergeant Shorter and the arrival of Jock Mercer I was left in charge of 1 Squadron Stores and I quite enjoyed my little bit of independence. One of the gunners who found himself on 'light' duties was seconded to stores and helped me out during this period. Phil Shuter was the man in question and Phil was a very enthusiastic scholar of the Roman army, its conquests and troop layout. By the time he left I was well versed in cohorts, praetorians, centurions and the fighting skills of a Roman soldier. It was very interesting but I didn't think knowing how to form shields to stave off arrows was going to be a lot of use to me in 1 LAA! It therefore came as a surprise when my next little jaunt included shields!

The local civilian workers on the camp had gone on strike for some reason or other and were picketing the main gates. The initial peaceful protest gradually turned a bit violent, although the local police seemed less than keen to intervene in what was quickly becoming a case of civil unrest. The bus that transported the married Australian airmen on to the camp was subjected to a regular barrage of eggs and abuse which threatened to turn into something far more serious if nothing was done to prevent it.

The camp commanding officer, an Australian, opted to leave his soldiers from 111 Battery, Royal Australian Artillery in peace and ordered 1 LAA Squadron Royal Air Force Regiment to go and restore law and order. Riot drill was quickly organised and a practice riot was arranged in a secluded part of the airfield. The riot squad were equipped with shields, batons and tear gas. All they wanted now was a bunch of rioters to practice their skills on.

"Taff, stick a scarf around your head or something. You're going to be a crazed rioter!"

"But I don't think I really want to be a crazed rioter, Sam," I replied nervously because I just knew, in my heart of hearts, that someone was going to get hurt somewhere along the line.

"Look," said Sam in a fairly reasonable tone of voice, "you can either be a crazed rioter or a bored guardroom inmate so fucking get out there."

THE RIOT SQUAD MOVE IN WITH INTENT TO HARM!

The riot squad were already lined up when we rioters turned up and they looked suitably menacing. Tin hats, riot shields, big batons, tear gas canisters etc. I wasn't aware at the time that tear gas was involved and this proved to be a bit unfortunate a little later on. Corporal of Gun, Sam was to be head rioter and we'd all been given loads of tomatoes and various objects to hurl, including the odd small brick we found lying about. Our instructions were to be as violent as we liked without actually wading into the squad. They, in turn, were ordered not to retaliate in any way initially and were allowed only to use their shields to ward off flying objects. This sounded like great fun to me and adrenaline overtook common sense as

Sam, with a scream of, "Give us more rice you English bastards," led us in a charge of wondrous ferocity. We had a whale of a time, chucking tomatoes and hollering like maniacs. It didn't last of course. The next thing I became aware of was a couple of canisters flying out of the ranks of the riot squad and going over our heads to land behind us. They were trailing what I took to be smoke.

SEE IF A BIT OF TEAR GAS WILL DO THE TRICK

Then, on a word of command, the squad started to move forward menacingly and I have to say, they looked ready to do some harm for all the rubbish we'd chucked at them. I backed away rapidly with all the others until Sam grabbed me by the arm and threw me forward again. This put me way too close to the advancing riot squad and I decided that was enough for me.

I turned and ran – straight into a cloud of what I very quickly discovered was tear gas. The effect was horrendous. It went in my mouth, nose, eyes and every other opening it could find. I was blinded by tears, choking and gasping for breath. I went down on one knee and was vaguely aware of the riot squad right in front of me.

"Thank Christ for that," I remembered thinking, "Be alright now. The lads will look after me and lead me gently away to safety…" In the event they marched right over me and even gave me a few gentle taps with their batons in passing. Bastards that they all were. I complained about this because I thought it was a bit over the bloody top. It was only practice after all and to act like thugs was totally out of order as far as I was concerned. It didn't do any good though. I was told that as far as they were concerned I could fuck off and die…!

In the event, the protesters abandoned their vigil and went back to work before all that practice could be put to use. I put it down to them catching sight of me after being gassed and clubbed. If the squad could do that in practice to one of their own, what in God's name were they likely to do when the real thing took place!

CHAPTER 8

A BIT OF MID-AIR MAYHEM

Shortly after my move to 1 LAA I took up parachuting with the Penang Services Parachute Club based at Bayan Lepas Airfield. In charge was Warrant Officer Bob Milligan of the Royal Australian Air Force (RAAF). Bob was ex Army and just about the toughest man I ever came across. He was a good man though and his rough humour and no nonsense way of running the club was terrific. He could play merry hell with you if you did something wrong but he could also be one of the most understanding of men if things went awry.

Before my first jump the one thing that terrified me more than anything else was 'bottling' it at the last moment. I didn't want to be thought of as a coward. Bob soon put us right about that.

"It doesn't require guts to jump out of an aeroplane," he told us during training one day, "Just a certain amount of stupidity! If I hear anyone even talking about someone bottling it I'll bloody jump all over them, is that clear?"

Absolutely crystal we all agreed.

There were quite a few Australian gunners from 111 Battery in the club and they were good lads to have around. A couple of them were highly experienced parachutists and the sprogs among us were well looked after. A couple of the regiment lads joined us and one of them, Ron Taylor, became a good friend of mine during our time both on the squadron and in the parachute club. It was an exciting time and I don't think anything quite gives you the thrill of plummeting earthwards, praying to God your parachute is going to open before you make a big dent in the airfield!

Things didn't always work out as planned but none of us ended up as fatalities, not while I was there at least. Some bruised ribs perhaps and a lot of limping after a hard landing sometimes but nothing that saw us being stretchered off the field of play as it were. I even managed to bugger things up on my first jump when I made a complete balls up of the landing. I forgot to turn the canopy around as I approached the ground and this manoeuvre had been drummed into us during training so there was no excuse really. Turning the canopy around to face into wind would slow down your descent prior to landing and ease you gently to the ground for a pain free arrival back on Mother Earth. That's what we were led to believe anyway. I never managed it and believe me, I tried. Not turning the canopy ensured you were thrown bodily into the ground like a sack of spuds being chucked off a hayloft. The level of violence involved when I struck the ground was horrendous. All the wind was knocked out of me and I sported some lovely bruises over my rib cage for days afterwards.

"Serves you right, Robert," sympathised Bob (he always called me Robert when he was tense) "If you'd fucking paid attention when I was wasting my breath talking to you it wouldn't have fucking hurt so much would it?"

Was I ever going to get any sympathy during my time in the Far East?

The parachutes we used in those days were slightly modified Irvin parachutes as used by the military. They were basic 'umbrella' shaped canopies (28ft circular canopies) and nothing near as advanced as the parachutes you see today. They had two guide toggles which allowed you to spin the 'chute around and this gave you a bit of manoeuvrability to allow you to make an attempt to get as close as possible to the landing zone marker cross. We received instruction on packing our own parachutes and for this we used the Parachute Packing Section at Butterworth camp. Bob Milligan was in charge of the section and it was, as ever, an entertaining way to learn a vital role in the field of parachuting. Three of us were in there one day undergoing instruction. We were to make our first descent the following week and were diligently following Bob's instructions. Fold the canopy over in sections, carefully separate the rigging, gently insert the split pins that would initially hold everything in and, vitally, make sure they were secured by easily breakable thread. Terrible stories had been told about one parachutist in Singapore who'd used nylon thread and spent a very uncomfortable few minutes dangling behind a Cessna before being cut loose to come down on his emergency 'chute.

I'd just about finished packing a parachute and Bob came over for a quick glance. He looked very serious as he poked about and hefted it in the air.

"Are you happy this is safely packed, Robert," he said, which I didn't like the sound of because I wanted *him* to tell me that it was safely packed!

"Yes, I think so," I replied which was a round about way of asking him to make bloody sure it was.

"Fair enough, mate. I hope it is because that's the 'chute you'll be using next week for your first jump!"

Oh, *Jesus Christ...!*

We learned how to deal with landing in the sea and we learned how to deal with a tree landing. Both eventualities didn't bare thinking about to be honest and the instruction we received was alarming to say the least.

"If youse is descending under your parachute and you notice that there's lots of trees where your airfield's supposed to be it's safe to assume that youse is in the wrong fucking place," started our lecture. It didn't get much better either but it boiled down to crossing your wrists in front of your face to prevent injury to the eyes, bending your knees to cushion the blow of hitting a large branch and praying to God that the tree was taller than your deployed parachute. This meant you'd get snagged by a friendly branch and be brought to a reasonably gentle halt before smashing through the branches and breaking both your legs when you struck the ground...

If it looked like you were going to land in the Penang Straits then you were in real trouble. The waters were full of poisonous sea snakes, huge jelly fish and plenty of other nasties. We'd been warned at the outset that it wasn't the wisest place for a bit of recreational swimming. However we had to know what to do if the worse happened.

"Unclip your harness and sit in it until you're close to getting your feet wet. Then jump out of it and start swimming," came the words of wisdom. "Be very careful though because it's very easy to misjudge height when you're over water. Jump too soon and you'll think you've landed on concrete. Jump too late and the canopy will land on top of you and drag you down. Either way will cause you a lot of grief so try not to land in the fucking sea."

End of lesson.

All of my jumps took place whilst I was serving on 1 LAA and there were plenty more alarming incidents to come. Life on the squadron moved on though and by now I was settled and happy in my new role. It was a long time since I'd been bored with my job and I threw myself into squadron life with enthusiasm. Sometimes this tended to work against me.

CHAPTER 9

THE DEMO TEAM

"How'd you fancy being on the Helicopter Demo Team?" I was asked one sun baked morning, "Nobody from HQ flight's volunteered so far."

Ooooooh! Yeah. Put me down for that please. Sounds fun. Which it was but there were bits of it that weren't fun as well. In fact, there were lots of bits that weren't fun at all.

First practice. Butterworth airfield. Flying Officer McGinness in charge.

I think there were about six of us on the team plus the Boss. The majority were 'rocks' with two of us being penguins (the other was an MT lad attached to the Squadron). The role of the team was to demonstrate to the Malay army how to deploy from a helicopter and for this we were to fly down to a base near Kuala Lumpur. The deployment techniques were to be in three stages. The first would see the helicopter land for our deployment, the second would have it hovering about five feet above the ground and the third stage had it fairly high up in the air to enable us to demonstrate roping down for deployment. No problem so far.

The RAAF provided the helicopter, a Huey and this duly turned up for our practice session. We practiced deploying throughout the afternoon and it was going quite well apart from the fact that I was a bit slow getting down the rope. Well, it wasn't easy was it? Bloody great thick rope like that and me with my delicate penguin hands. I soon got the hang of it though and was starting to enjoy myself, which was a mistake all on its own. In addition to the rifles we were carrying one of the boys carried a radio on his back which was quite heavy and cumbersome. The MT penguin was given the task of carrying it and he was having a few problems. On about the third practice he was last out of the Huey as the rest of us watched from the ground. I was alongside Flying Officer McGinness as the tragedy unfolded. I could see this lad was a bit hesitant but then he just went for it. He wrapped his legs around the rope and grabbed it with both hands.

Whether he was just tired from all the practice or whether his strength failed him I don't know but whatever it was it caused him to come sliding down the rope at a sickening speed. He let out a cry of agony and crashed to the ground in a tangle of legs, rifle, radio and shredded hands from the rope burn. They were a bloody mess and it was obvious we wouldn't be seeing him on the team again. Naturally (that word again) most of us laughed. I don't know why we laughed. Perhaps it was just nerves or perhaps it was just genuinely funny to our particular brand of regiment humour.

BELL UH-1 IROQUOIS (HUEY) HELICOPTER

"You think that's funny do you, Price?" Flying Officer McGinness asked me in a none too friendly tone. "Well, here's another laugh for you. Go and take the radio off him. You'll be carrying it from now on."

Now hold on just a minute here. You've already told me I'm slow on the rope and now you want me to stick half a ton of radio on my back which isn't really going to make me move

any faster is it. Doesn't make a lot of fucking sense really, does it? I didn't actually say that of course but at least I was allowed to think it. For those of you who want the full version of events the words I actually used were, "Yes, sir."
I was beginning to learn how not to make a bad situation worse!

FLYING OFFICER McINNESS BRIEFING SOLDIERS OF THE MALAY ARMY

Our first trip to Kuala Lumpur was quite enjoyable and all went well with the demonstration. I was just happy to get down the rope with skin still on my hands and both legs intact. Our efforts were appreciated though and when we'd finished our demonstration we were offered the chance to have a go at the army's jungle firing range. This was great fun due to the fact that it wasn't a standard range. The targets were various objects tied to tree branches and we got to blast away to our hearts content. Then it was up and away back to Butterworth for a few beers. More than a few to be honest but we felt we deserved it. The second time we went down there we were given a different Australian pilot and that's when things got totally out of hand.

'MADE IT MA – TOP OF THE WORLD'
THE BOSS DEMONSTRATES THE WINCHING TECHNIQUE

As we headed towards the Huey for the trip back to base I could see it was sat facing the jungle which was quite close to our location. Between the Huey and the jungle stood a huge tree that must have been there a very long time. It was massive. I strapped myself in, facing forward, behind the pilot. I naturally assumed he'd lift the Huey gently off the ground and turn away from the tree or maybe take it up vertically until he was over the top of it. Why I assumed that I've no idea. Perhaps I thought Australian helicopter pilots were a bit timid and reserved!

The rotor blades stirred into life with a whine and we lifted gently into the air. I had a lovely view out of the front windshield. Suddenly the nose dropped down and we were almost vertical to the ground. All I could see through the front screen was wall to wall grass. Then the Huey leapt forward on full power and screamed straight at the tree. The view through the screen changed from wall to wall grass to wall to wall tree and I had a terrifyingly fleeting thought that I was about to die. I was genuinely convinced that we just couldn't miss smashing straight into it. Then the Huey went from nose down vertical to nose up vertical and I was viewing yet another change of scenery. Wall to wall sky this time. I don't suppose the whole incident took more than ten seconds but I lived a lifetime in those horrendous few moments. When everything settled down I took a quick look at the other lads and, it has to be said, they didn't look like hardened rock apes with devil may care grins on their faces either.

"Amazing what these things can do isn't it, boys," came from the comedian in the driver's seat, who seemed to be enjoying himself hugely. I'm not sure if he saw any of the hate filled looks aimed at him from the back seat passengers but if he did, he ignored them.

I'd have settled for a quiet ride back to camp after that performance but that didn't happen either. The Huey suddenly plunged earthwards and began to follow the coastline at a height I'd guess at no more than fifty feet. It has to be said that it was thrilling and a bit of an adrenaline rush as we looked down on fishing boats and startled, upturned faces from the villages we roared over. For pure excitement it couldn't be bettered. It wasn't the end of it though. In a bizarre episode we set down on a golf course!

"I've got a mate here, fellers," says our pilot. "Hop out and have a smoke. I'll be back in half an hour."
I'm not sure what the golfers thought when they saw a Huey sat on the green with all of us sat smoking under its shadow but it's

a safe bet that they'd never come across a hazard like that before. Beats a sand bunker all ends up!

THE HELICOPTER DEMO TEAM 1966   (THE AUTHOR IS FAR RIGHT)

My time with the team was hugely enjoyable. I enjoyed the excitement and, of more importance to me, the way I was accepted by the regiment lads. None of them treated me as though I was a passenger and I appreciated this. I was afforded no favours due to my penguin status nor did I ask for any. I felt comfortable being in the company of regiment gunners both on duty and off. It was to stand me in good stead for the rest of my time on the squadron.

CHAPTER 10

THAT'S OUR BLOODY GUN

Life wasn't all duty of course and we had our fair share of off duty mayhem. Most of us were still single and as far as I can recall none of us had taken vows of abstinence or chastity! To young men still in their teens or twenties Penang Island was Shangri La as far as we were concerned. The bars naturally attracted servicemen like light attracts moths and the other places where rest and recuperation were on offer usually had a beaming 'Mamasan' on hand to welcome us. All very hospitable of course.

We also had the NAAFI on Butterworth Camp and it was here that this next incident took place. I've no idea what the occasion was but 1 LAA were in full attendance and, as usual, things were bordering on chaos by the end of the night. I was stood outside enjoying a quiet smoke and a bit of solitude when suddenly a three tonner towing a Bofors gun went hurtling past on the road nearby. The next thing I'm aware of is Sergeant of Gun Harry lurching out of the NAAFI and hanging on to me.

"That's our fucking gun, Taff," he belched, "Those Australian bastards have stolen our gun!"

To make things a bit clearer both 1 LAA and the Australian 111 Battery were equipped with Bofors. 1 Squadron had the 40/70s whilst 111 Battery had the 40/60s.

"How'd you know it's our gun, Harry?" I asked him in a reasonable manner.

"Think I don't know one of our own fucking guns," he snarls and went back inside to recruit volunteers to go and get it back. He was gone a long time and when he came back out he was alone. I guessed that nobody cared too much about this gun. It didn't seem to put him off though because he lurched off in hot pursuit on his own. I went back inside and told everyone still capable of understanding that he'd gone off to the Australian barracks to get the gun back.

"S'good of him," was about the most coherent reply I could get and we all promptly forgot about him. I never did find out what happened because he didn't come back. I suspect he probably failed in his objective!

Not long after this incident one of the gunners came in to my stores for a chat and a smoke. Jock Mercer was out at the time which was a bit of a shame because he might have been able to prevent what happened.

"You heard anything about us being posted to Borneo, Taff," I was asked in conversational tone. I replied that, no, nothing had been mentioned to me and that was it. After my gossip mongering mate had left one of the sergeants came in for something or other and I asked him if he'd heard anything about the squadron being posted to Borneo. He looked a bit alarmed about this and began to question me as to where I'd got the information before dashing off at speed. To explain a bit about the situation out in the Far East at the time, a conflict known as the Indonesian Confrontation was ongoing. In 1963 Indonesia's President Sukharno had vowed to crush Malaysia and set off a chain of events that would see armed conflict rage for three long years. It ended in August 1966 when the two countries signed an accord ending the hostilities. Borneo bore the brunt of the fighting and it wasn't a fun place to be posted so I was told.

Warrant Officer Frank Sylvester was the next man to appear and he told me to accompany him to the commanding officer's lair. A bit alarmed but not unduly worried I went with him and stood in front of Squadron Leader Adams who was flanked by two of his officers.

"Who told you we were going to Borneo?" he asked with an edge to his voice.

"Nobody told me sir. One of the lads asked me if I'd heard anything about us going that's all," I replied in haste. He then gave me a sustained bollocking about rumour mongering and its implications and told me that all it needed was for someone at HQ to pick up on it and decide that sending us to Borneo wasn't a bad idea after all.

"Do you want to go to Borneo?" he ended and I thought it was a genuine question not a threat. I made the mistake of hesitating slightly which I think he took to mean that I wouldn't mind going and this was wrong as well apparently! He made a couple of dire threats and muttered something to Frank Sylvester about taking me away and hurting me but he had the grace to give a small smile as he said it – only a very small smile but a smile anyway. Frank marched me out, had a few choice words with me and sent me back to stores. I wouldn't have minded but as far as I was concerned I couldn't see what I'd done wrong. I complained to Jock Mercer when he came back but he just laughed. So much for the solidarity of storemen. We never did get posted to Borneo so why they went on about it I don't know!

Life moved on as it tended to do and I found that whenever something was going on I was usually involved. I put it down to being a real squadron asset whilst everyone else put it down to a shortage of available gunners who were all manning the gun positions and OPs! Sometimes this was good and sometimes it wasn't so good.

News came in one day of three missing sailors in the Penang Straits. It was feared they'd gone into the water but a search revealed no bodies. It was felt they may have been washed ashore and 1 Squadron was given the task of searching the beach area on the Butterworth side of the Straits. I found myself in a line of gunners moving down the beach looking for the body. I was on the end of the line closest to the sea whilst the rest of the lads were strung out beside me up the beach and into the edge of the undergrowth.

We'd gone a fair way down the beach when a halt was called and I stood idly looking out to sea. My boots were very close to the water and I had a quick glance down to make sure I wasn't in danger of getting my feet wet. I can only describe the next moment as one that almost stopped my heart! Less than a foot from my boot one of the most hideous snakes I've ever seen in my life lay in the shallows. The water was very clear that close in and I saw every single scale and glittering eyes of this hideous monster. I think I jumped at least five feet sideways with a shout of alarm.

I think everyone thought I'd spotted a body and came down for a shuftee as you'd expect. The sea snake's body was squat and thick with an awful diamond shaped head that looked positively demonic. My heart was thumping still and I told our leader that if it was all the same to him I'd like to take a turn searching the other end of the line for a change. Some wildlife expert was of the opinion that if the snake was that far into the shallows it was probably dead but nobody seemed keen on giving it a prod to find out and it was left well alone. We all knew that sea snakes were highly venomous and even if it was dead it could still retain a reflex bite action if poked about the head. Nobody poked it about the head either!

"GO ON. POKE IT IN THE HEAD TO SEE IF IT'S STILL ALIVE."

I was moved to the other end of the line amid much jeering and chicken clucking sounds but I just didn't care. I didn't want to come across anything like that again. Eventually we moved on down the beach until we came across a sort of marshy area. Because it was furthest away from the sea it was only in front of two of us at that end of the line and we duly moved down a bit to avoid wading through it. Seemed sensible to me and Fred, the other lad, but it didn't seem to please our leader.

"You can just fucking well get back up there and search that area," he ordered.

Now I wished I'd stayed by the sea. Fred looked at me and he wasn't smiling happily, I can tell you that much.

"Fucking hell, Taff. There's snakes and all sorts of bloody things in swamps," he comforted me. I'd have preferred him not to call it a swamp because that just served to dredge up images of Tarzan films with crocodiles and large snakes slithering through them. Both of us gently stepped forward though and thankfully we only sank in up to just above our ankles. This stretch of marshy ground was only about a hundred feet across and we went through it in about twenty seconds, max!

"And now you can fucking well go back and do that again," came an outraged cry, "and this time walk through it and have a feel about with your feet like you're fucking well supposed to do."

Which we did of course. No sense upsetting him any further after all.

We never did find the bodies but they eventually washed ashore and were recovered for a decent burial. A sad end for three brave lads.

CHAPTER 11

MORE AIRBORNE ANTICS

The parachuting was still ongoing and this was no less incident free than life on the squadron. Ron Taylor made a name for himself when he moved forward a bit too eagerly one day whilst on the run in to the exit point. Bob Milligan was sat behind him, holding on to his static line ready to feed it out as Ron got on to the wing and the sudden movement ripped open a couple of the ties, partially releasing the parachute. Bob was cradling handfuls of canopy and calling for the pilot to abort and head back to the airfield when Ron made a suggestion that he be allowed to jump anyway. In return he received a suggestion that had nothing whatsoever to do with parachuting!

ALL I WANTED FOR CHRISTMAS...

WITH RON TAYLOR (RIGHT) JUST BEFORE 4TH DESCENT.

The club was then asked to do a couple of demonstration jumps at Alor Star and one of our regiment members, Pilot Officer Steve Breretom-Martin arranged for several of us to fly down with all the kit in a DC3 (Dakota). We managed to turn up late and the DC3 was already on the runway, engines revving for take off. Steve directed the driver to stop at the control tower and dashed upstairs to ask them to hold the aircraft until we got there. We roared out to the Dakota where the back door was being held open for us, chucked in all our gear, clambered off the back of the land rover and fell into the cabin. That was it. The door was slammed shut and we were rolling down the runway before we'd even managed to get strapped into our seats. Impatient buggers those Australian pilots!

The demonstration went well and we stayed overnight for a very pleasant stay before heading back to Butterworth. The same DC3 was going to pick us up but this time it had a couple of VIPs on board. One of them was a very high ranking RAF officer and the other his lovely wife. Two very comfortable chairs had been bolted into the front of the aircraft for their journey whilst the rest of us were strapped into not so comfortable parachute seats at the back. All our parachutes were dumped on the floor in front of us. There was quite a torrential downpour going on as we took off and the tail of the DC3 was slewing sideways wildly in the wind. Then the back door sprang open whilst we were no more than fifty feet up. To alleviate your fears for our safety it didn't slam wide open to crash against the fuselage but it went as far as the hinges allowed it. That however, was far enough for me to see the tree tops not so far below and the gusting squalls of rain lashing across them. The noise as the wind shrieked through the gap was enough to make your teeth hurt.

The air quartermaster came charging down the cabin, strapped himself in and leaned out to grab hold of the door handle. After a tense struggle he managed to get it shut again. Well, fair enough. That was exciting but let's not do that again in a hurry please. We settled in for the flight and before long the quartermaster came back with a large slice of cake for all of us, courtesy of the lady up front who was celebrating her birthday. Both she and her husband turned to give us a friendly wave. A very pleasant gesture.

AUTHOR IS FAR LEFT, PETER AND STEVE (AUSTRALIAN 111 BATTERY) IN THE MIDDLE AND STEVE BRERETOM MARTIN (1 LAA) ON THE RIGHT. THIS TAKEN JUST BEFORE TAKE OFF FROM ALOR STAR. THE OFFENDING DOOR CAN BE SEEN ON THE DC3!

"How many jumps have you done so far, Price," I was asked by the flight lieutenant in charge of the squadron parachute flight as I walked by his office one day.

"Six so far, sir, "I replied, "be seven after tomorrow."

A couple of days later, Ron Taylor came over to have a chat with me. He was seconded to the duty office at the time, helping out the Squadron clerk.

"D'you know your name's on the Parachute Flight list," he asked, which gave me quite a start. I thought he was being sarcastic but he insisted on taking me to have a look for myself and there it was in black and white with an annotation, 'Locally Free Fall Trained.' I was overjoyed and asked if I could have my wings and the extra pay but it didn't quite work like that. I'd need to go on a military parachute course in Singapore for that to happen and one was due very shortly. I approached the flight lieutenant organising the course and asked if I could sign up. He informed me that he'd be more than happy to take me along but it wasn't his decision. That could only be given by my own stores CO, Squadron Leader Arnold. I duly made out an application and sent it over for his attention, anticipating no problem.

"Now look, Price, I'm very sorry but I just can't authorise this course for you. For a start I've got to convince the powers that be that a parachute qualification is absolutely necessary for a supplier!"

I did my best to plead my case but it did no good and I was bitterly disappointed. Ron Taylor and several others from 1 Squadron went down for the course and came back with their wings and smug expressions on their chops. I've never got over it and one of my mates actually wrote to 1 Squadron a couple of years back to ask if they could put a stop to my moaning and send me a set of wings. They told him to bugger off! What a way to treat an honorary rock ape!

By this time the Green Jackets had been posted in and several of them joined us, making a nice, varied mix of servicemen. One of them was to give me the most memorable sight of my life and it was incredible. It was at another demonstration jump and I'd gone up with one of the Green Jackets who was wearing a bright orange jump suit. He was free fall qualified and the idea was for me to go out first on the static line and for him to follow me out, dropping past me before opening his parachute. My own 'chute opened just in time for me to see him plummeting past me in free fall. He was quite close and the sight of this brightly dressed figure hurtling past me with his 'chute streaming out behind him was amazing. It became etched on my memory and I can conjure it up to this day. Unfortunately, so did the next bit!

To liven the demonstration up a bit thunder flashes were given to the more experienced jumpers and these were dropped whilst they were in mid air. All very exciting but then some lunatic came up with a bright idea for the rest of us who weren't allowed to chuck these things about the sky.

"NOW WHAT WAS IT AGAIN?"
" LEGS TOGETHER, KNEES BENT."

"The ground party can chuck them in the air beneath you as you come down," he said with unhinged enthusiasm. Oh yeah, who's going to chuck them up then? Why, the Green Jackets of course. Now don't get me wrong. They were lovely lads and I had some good friends among them but health and safety was something none of them had ever heard of. In fact it was positively discouraged in their regiment. The upshot of this dangerous idea was that I had thunder flashes exploding all over the place as I was descending. I thought they'd stop when I got in chucking distance. I thought they might be concerned they'd set my parachute alight. Apparently not because these things began to explode ever closer as I slowly descended.

"For fuck's sake, pack it in," I managed to holler before the necessary matter of landing safely suddenly took my attention elsewhere. I thought there'd be an apology somewhere along the line. I don't really know why. My penguin sensitivity probably hadn't quite been extinguished by 1 LAA at the time. In the event, no apology was received and I'm pretty certain none was considered necessary either.

There were two things in our little world of airborne woe that were considered worthy of a death sentence! One was to pick up your reserve parachute by the 'D' ring instead of the carrying handle and the other was to lose your 'D' ring. A 'D'ring is exactly that. A 'D' shaped piece of metal attached to the 'rip cord' used to release your canopy when in free fall mode. The usual time span to convert from the static line (which used to open the 'chute automatically) to free fall was as long as it took you to carry out seven drops on the static line or until you were considered safe enough to open your own 'chute. Usually jumps six and seven were used for dummy pulls. The static line would still open your 'chute but a dummy 'D' ring, minus rip cord, would be inserted in its housing to allow you to practice pulling it in real time.

On jump six I was duly fitted with a dummy 'D' ring and given my instructions.

"One thousand – look down to locate 'D' ring, two thousand – right arm in to grasp 'D'ring whilst left arm comes across to maintain stability – three thousand – pull 'D' ring out with right hand and throw both arms back out in full spread position to keep stability. Worked like a dream but what to do with the 'D' ring now I had it clutched in my hot little hand? I needed both hands free to turn the parachute for landing. No problem. Stick it behind my reserve 'chute. Should be safe there.

This landing was going to be a bit different though. We were at a place called Ipoh if memory serves correct and our drop zone was on the far side of the airfield. It was also quite close to some big trees and a marshy piece of rock strewn ground. I'd gone off course somewhere along the line (I blamed gusting winds on this occasion) and could see the trees starting to look uncomfortably close. I didn't fancy a tree landing and managed to turn away from them at the last minute to land in the marshes. I was wet and soggy but grateful not to have hit any of the rocks. I came down like a ton of bricks as usual and everything that could move, moved and everything that could rattle, rattled.

As I struggled out on to dry ground like something from the Black Lagoon I was met with the usual sensible remarks from the ground party.

"What you doing in there, Taff?"

"Landing cross is over there mate. Bit small for you is it?"

"Made a right fucking mess of that didn't you!"

This wasn't unusual though and I shrugged it off with a sulk. Then I discovered my 'D' ring was missing! When I unclipped my reserve it had gone. It must have fallen out when I landed. I'd committed the cardinal sin.

"Better get back in there," smirked one of the lads, "find it before Bob Milligan comes over and goes fucking berserk!"

As far as I'm aware, that 'D' ring could still be buried out there to this day. Bob was quite good about it though. Called me a bloody pommie idiot as a prelude to a proper bollocking and that was it. A week later I picked up my reserve 'chute by the

'D' ring instead of the carrying handle and watched helplessly as the canopy spilled out and unravelled all over the airfield at Bayan Lepas. Two major sins in two weeks. Ah, well, things could only get better.

Which, as a matter of fact, they didn't!

CHAPTER 12

IT'S ONLY BLOOD!

I wouldn't have said I was squeamish during my time with 1 LAA, apart from my aversion to needles and snakes that is. The sight of blood didn't worry me too much other than when it was my own and this proved to be my undoing.

This time it was another jungle experience exercise. An ambush exercise to be precise and I went into it with an unhealthy eagerness. I'd be getting all the excitement of being under fire but without the danger. I could face up to a barrage of bullets being shot my way, safe in the knowledge that they were all blanks and quite harmless. The first hint that things weren't going to go as planned came when Corporal 'Taff' Evans told me I was going to be his radio man for the exercise.

"But I don't know how to operate the radio, Taff," I objected.

"For Christ's sake, all you've got to do is press a button and say what I bloody tell you to say," he replied kindly. "You carried it on the helicopter team didn't you so you'll be used to it won't you."

I hefted this thing on to my back and picked up my rifle. I wasn't happy that I'd be lugging it all over the place but I didn't complain. That would only have cheered everyone up and I didn't want to give them the satisfaction. To start the exercise off our patrol would be the 'victims' of an ambush and for the first part we'd be in the back of a three tonner that

Corporal 'Taff' Evans (middle) with his trusty radio man!

would drive part way into the jungle on a bit of driveable track. It took a bit of heaving to get me up into the vehicle but I just knew, in my heart of hearts, that it wouldn't take any effort at all to get me back out of it!

A crackle of rifle fire broke the air and a cry of, "*AMBUSH, RIGHT*" had the three tonner skidding to a halt and everyone leaping out to take cover on the left hand side of the track. My orders were quite simple.

"Stick very close to Corporal Evans and try not to fuck things up!"

Both of us were kneeling down in a ditch looking up at a hillside where the firing had come from. This was also where the exercise umpires were placed. Another outbreak of firing came and I was itching to let off a few rounds. I already had my rifle at the aim towards the hill but I don't think Taff noticed it at the time. He was busy trying to locate the 'enemy.'

A movement on the hillside caught my attention and Taff put his arm behind him to slap me on the shoulder.

"There's one of the little bastards, Taff. Give it...."

He didn't get the chance to finish because I leaned right across him and fired off three shots in rapid succession. At least one of the casings went down his shirt front and I suppose it must have been a tad hot because he was slapping at his chest as though I'd put a live round into him! There was a bit of a scene, as you'd expect and we must have exposed our position because the next thing we hear is a plummy voice calling, "You, Corporal. You're dead and so is your radio man!"

"Oh, for *fuck's* sake," snarled Taff, looking at me in disgust. At least we had time for a smoke whilst we were 'dead' before moving on to the next stage of the exercise.

We moved deeper into the jungle for the next part and joined up with some of the other gunners. We ended up in a very dense part of undergrowth with more of the same ahead of us and the sweat was running off us at this point. We couldn't move forwards and it looked like the only sensible option would be to move back out of it. Then my radio crackled into life and one of the young pilot officers undergoing training came on the air. I can't remember what our call signs were but the conversation was along the lines of:

"Get your corporal to carry out a flanking manoeuvre in readiness to engage the enemy."

I alerted the corporal who was leading this part of the exercise that I'd just taken a message from the command post and told him what they wanted.

"Carry out a flanking manoeuvre?" he said incredulously, "We can't move three fucking feet in any direction, let alone carry out a fucking flanking manoeuvre. Give me the fucking mike."

There was a heated exchange over the airways that ended quite badly but the upshot was that we moved to clearer ground to carry on where we left off.

The exercise slowly wound down and we were all gathered together for a briefing on the final assault. The CO and several of the squadron officers had set up shop in a small clearing to direct the exercise and our finale was to have us lay down a thick layer of smoke and charge through it to end up in front of the CO and his merry men. All good stuff of course. Very exciting. We formed up and I had a few words with Bill Twist on my left, who was carrying a Bren gun. He was happily slapping a full magazine into the Bren and looked intent on making sure it was empty by the time he'd finished.

The smoke canisters erupted and a huge pall of thick smoke billowed into the air. It was like being engulfed in thick fog but we all charged through it, firing as fast as we could. I looked briefly to my left and saw Bill firing the Bren from the hip. Then he disappeared in a huge flash and bang that exploded between us. Thunder flashes. Nobody told me they'd be chucking thunder flashes at us and this one nearly deafened me. I reeled away from the flash and saw nothing else until we came out of the smoke to end the exercise.

I eased off my radio and propped my rifle against a tree. Out came the water bottles and fags for a well deserved break. Everyone was laughing and joking when Taff Evans suddenly appeared in front of me. What now, I thought. I didn't shoot him again did I!

"You okay, Taff?" he asked me with concern.

"Yes, fine thanks mate," I replied, "Why?"

"Because you've got blood pouring down your arm," he informed me. I looked quickly down and there was indeed blood pouring down my left arm. I hadn't felt a thing and to this day I don't know what caused it. Maybe it was the thunder flash but I didn't think they were meant to inflict damage, just make a lot of noise. Whatever it was it cut me quite badly and as soon as I caught sight of the blood I felt an urgent need to sit down before I fell down. I was quickly bandaged up and got the usual ribald sympathy from all my mates.

"Had to be the bloody penguin didn't it."

"Get up you lazy bastard. I'm not carrying you back."

"Don't bleed over the fucking radio either – it's not sanitary!"

There was plenty more of course and much hilarity. At least I got to go back to camp like a wounded soldier, all bandaged and bloodied. I kept the bandage on far longer than was necessary of course and displayed it like a badge of honour for at least a week. Nobody took a blind bit of notice so why I bothered I don't know. I fully believe I'd have got the same lack of attention if my arm had been blown off!

CHAPTER 13

A QUICK REALITY CHECK

I was enjoying life to the full out in the Far East. Everything was new and exciting. I made friends with quite a few Malay and Chinese lads while I was there and the different cultures among them I found fascinating. I quickly learned that it was considered very rude to beckon someone by waving them towards you with an upturned palm. The first time one of the Chinese lads called me over I thought he was shooing me away with his palm down gesture.

By the time I joined 1 LAA I was comfortable with life in a foreign land and got to know Penang Island very well indeed, both the tourist side and the seedier side! At the time we didn't consider the seedy side to be seedy at all and spent most of our off duty time there. When we weren't skint that is and that was more often than not.

One pay day a few of the regiment lads decided not to venture too far for the customary Tiger beer/disgraceful behaviour outing and I'd arranged to meet them in a bar near

Butterworth Ferry Port. I say bar but in reality it was little more than a shack with very basic comforts on hand. Nobody worried about that though. Providing the beer was cold and the glasses didn't have too many chips in them we were happy. I was going down on my motor bike to save on taxi fares and Scouse cadged a lift with the same aim in mind. When I picked him up he was in uniform.

"Where's your civvies, Scouse," I asked him.

"In the pawn shop. Had to hock them to get money for beer didn't I?" he replied.

"But it's bloody pay day. Don't tell me you're fucking skint already?" I said.

"Yeah, by the time I paid off my debts I was left with about five dollars," he said ruefully. As we were paid every two weeks out there I feared Scouse was in for a very lean fortnight.

The local pawn shop did a roaring trade from servicemen and my lovely Olympus Pen EE camera spent more time there than it did in my possession. When I came back home the customs officer in London refused to believe it was over two years old because it was in such pristine condition. Cigarettes were usually bought in bulk to see us through but nobody went without a smoke if their mates had one to spare.

I was content with my lot it has to said. Life was good and nearly everything, good or bad, was treated with a laugh, even some of the grimmer stuff. I think I'd become a little bit too complacent and, as usual, life could be relied on to come up out of nowhere and slap you around a bit to take the smile off your face.

In February 1966 a Royal Air Force Jet Provost, conducting trials over the Malayan jungle, crashed in a remote area near a place called Alor Star. The pilot failed to eject in time and was killed on impact. 1 LAA was immediately mobilised to go out to the aircraft and put a guard on it. This meant a long journey by road before going off road onto some inhospitable jungle tracks and finally to the crash site deep in the jungle. I opened up our stores and issued all the kit required by the advance party. It was all done at a frantic pace and they were gone in minutes. My request to go with them was turned down flat.

"We don't have time to wait for you. Ask the CO if you can come out with him in the morning."

I turned up bright and early the next morning in my jungle greens and took the liberty of signing out a rifle in readiness. My SMG stayed in the armoury. Too much hassle sorting out different ammunition I was told. Everyone in the advance party had gone out armed and I thought it might save a bit of time. The CO was going up in the land rover with one of the pilot officers and a couple of other gunners. I presented myself in front of him and asked if I could go along for the experience. No problem, hop in, off we go…

It was a long journey and part of it took us down a very long, dusty road. It was a very fine, red dust and it got everywhere. It stuck to the sweat on our bodies, it stuck to our clothes, it got in the rifle barrels and it put a nice red tan on our faces. I dread to think what we looked like but it felt awful and itched like Hell. When we got to the jungle part of the track we went through a Malay village and the CO called a halt to check the map. Looking out of the back of the land rover I saw a little old Malay man looking our way. He looked very old to me but then again, at age twenty, everyone over thirty five looked old!

"Price, you speak Malay don't you?" said the CO, catching me off guard. The truth was, I'd been to about three lessons before giving it up but told everybody I had a smattering of the language. This basically boiled down to, 'good morning,' 'good afternoon,' 'good night' and 'Two large beers please!'

"A bit, sir," I replied cautiously.

"Well, go and ask that chap if he knows where the aircraft went down or if he saw our advance party come through."

Oh, great! Here's where I make an absolute balls up of things. I went to get out of the land rover and then had my rifle snatched out of my hands.

"And don't threaten him with a bloody rifle either for Christ's sake…and be polite."

I don't know why he felt the need to say that because I was always polite but then again it was probably best to be reminded. I walked up to the old man and bade him good morning with a smile. That was almost a quarter of my Malay vocabulary used up for a start. He smiled back because they were a very friendly race and returned my greeting. We were far enough away from the Land Rover not to be heard and I thought I might just get away with it by using hand gestures and a bit of pigeon English. I must have sounded like the village idiot because this lovely old man suddenly put his hand on my arm, leaned in and said quietly, "It's alright young man, I speak English quite well!"

God bless this tactful, educated man. He was able to point me in the right direction as taken by the advance party the previous day. I thanked him profusely and went back to report to the CO.

"Well done, Price. It pays to have someone who speaks the language doesn't it," he said warmly.

"Absolutely, sir," I said without blushing. Well, it wasn't often I got a bit of praise and I felt I ought to make the most of it while I could!

We eventually pulled up at the crash site and climbed out of the Land Rover. The Jet Provost could just about be seen up a hill amongst the trees. The CO was going up to the aircraft with a couple of the others and I asked if I could go as well. He hesitated before telling me that it might be best if I didn't. The body of the pilot had been recovered from the cockpit but there were still some very gruesome remains inside.

"On second thoughts," the CO suddenly said, "It might do you a bit of good. Come on then."
I don't know why he thought it might do me a bit of good. Perhaps he thought it might knock my rose tinted glasses off and show me that life wasn't all fun. It did that all right.

THE REMAINS OF THE JET PROVOST

As we approached the aircraft through the undergrowth it felt very still and ominous. The heat was stifling and the smell terrible. Swarms of flies were buzzing about all over the place. The aircraft was buried nose down and the first thing that struck me was the small drogue parachute wrapped around the tail plane. Whether the pilot made a last second attempt to eject from the doomed plane or whether it activated on impact I've no idea. We walked up to the cockpit and looked inside. It was an awful sight. One I'd never like to see again and, despite the heat, I shivered involuntarily. A graphic description of the scene isn't necessary. Suffice to say that a very brave man lost his life in that crash and may he rest in peace.

We went back down to where the advance party had set up shop and the boys all crowded around to welcome us. I didn't think I was that popular but it turned out all they were interested in was the contents of my water bottle. They must have been short on drinking water because, before I knew it, my bottle was empty and I went thirsty for the rest of the day! There wasn't any grub on offer either so I went hungry as well. When we got back to Butterworth and dropped the CO off we went straight up the bar and knocked back a couple of pints of cold Tiger. Very unwise but to be honest I wasn't in the mood for healthy living lectures at the time and they went down a treat.

It was a rewarding experience. One I wouldn't like to repeat but I'm grateful to Squadron Leader Adams for giving me the opportunity. If his aim was to teach me that life wasn't all fun and games then he succeeded. I think maybe I started to grow up a little that day.

CHAPTER 14

A FEW MINOR TRIALS AND TRIBULATIONS

Life on the squadron was never dull and this suited me – sometimes! Quite often, when things were a bit slow in our stores, I'd sit at my desk and look out at the flight offices, idly noting the comings and goings of various people. Now and again I'd note one of them heading in my direction and this always led to a stirring of interest, wondering what was coming my way.

The view from my stores window
1 Squadron HQ Flight Butterworth 1966

On this particular day it was one of our corporals, Paddy, and he had a notebook in his grasp, studying it intently.

"Fancy a game of rugby, Taff?" he asked when he came in, "we're a bit short for a team."

"Who against, Paddy?" I asked

"Triple One Battery," (Australian Army) he replied. "It's only a friendly though. Couple of crates of beer being laid on for after the game. Nothing strenuous."

Like a fool I put my name down.

In the event we got slaughtered. The Australian goal kicker played in bare feet and kicked every penalty they were awarded whilst the rest of his team played as though their very lives depended on the outcome! My opposing wing forward took a personal delight in trying to maim me at every scrum and I came off the field at the end looking like I'd been in a car crash! Squadron Leader Adams was there to witness our humiliation of course but he seemed quite happy with things and had an encouraging word for all of us. The cold beer soon eased the aches and pains though and I even shook hands with the Aussie who'd spent the preceding eighty minutes trying to disfigure me.

One incident took place when I was between sergeants as it were and had been put temporarily in charge of our stores. I was walking across to the admin office when I heard a quiet voice call out from an adjacent office.

"Taff, come here a sec would you. We've got a problem."
Now this alarmed me for a couple of reasons because the voice belonged to one of our flight lieutenants. My first cause for alarm was the fact that he called me 'Taff' and not 'Price' or 'Oy, you' as was the norm. The second cause for alarm were the words, "We've got a problem," because as far as I was concerned I didn't have a problem but knew with absolute certainty that I was about to inherit one!

There were two of them in the office, poring over various inventory forms and looking a bit worried.

"For some reason we seem to be down about thirty bed sheets. God knows where they've gone. I don't suppose you could do anything about that could you?" came the hundred dollar question.
I knew I could. Quite easily as well but it wouldn't exactly be legal.

"I could sort that out, sir," I replied. "I'd need a vehicle and driver though and no questions asked."

His face clouded for a second before he said, "Okay. You can have the CO's Land Rover and driver but remember, if you get caught doing anything you shouldn't be doing, don't bloody mention my name…!"

To explain things about exchanging bedding. There was a bedding store over by the main stores building and one day a week was set aside to take in dirty sheets and have them replaced by freshly laundered items. The method used to take them in was simple. Spread out a sheet, dump all the dirty ones inside and bundle them up like a Christmas pud. I knew what it was like on sheet change day and I knew the Chinese lad, Jimmy Choo, who ran the store. Jimmy was a bit of a character and very overweight. He ran the store mostly on his own and on sheet change days it was mayhem. There'd be a mountain of bundled up dirty sheets piled up near the store entrance and this was how I intended to replace the ones 'lost' by 1 LAA.

Bill, the CO's driver, drove me over to the bedding store and parked up just around the corner, out of sight. He then accompanied me into the store and we went up to the counter where Jimmy was dishing out clean sheets.

"Herro, Taff, wha' you wan'?" he asked. I dumped about ten sheets down on the counter, the only ones we had left on the squadron, and asked Jimmy if he could change them for us.

"Course I can frucking change sheets. Wha' you think I here for?" He said, grinning at Bill. He waddled off around the back to get the clean sheets and I knew it'd take him at least five minutes to get back again. I grabbed a large bundle of dirty sheets from the big pile by the entrance and chucked them at Bill who disappeared at speed to dump them in the Land Rover. When Jimmy came back, he handed me the clean sheets, looked over my shoulder and said, "Where yo' frien' go?"

"He had to dash back to the squadron, Jim," I told him, "You know what these regiment types are like."
He seemed happy with that and I went off with my clean sheets. Bill had the engine running when I turned up and we set off back to the squadron at speed.

I'd earned my bonus points, the inventory was up to date and everyone was happy. Some may see this sort of thing as criminal or petty theft at the least but there was a bit of a code about things like that. If you took stuff and sold it for gain outside the RAF then that was theft and you deserved to have your hands chopped off but if you took it and put it somewhere else within the RAF that was re-distribution of stock. My conscience was clear!

There were times when we actually took stuff out of our stores and gave it away outside the RAF but that was fully authorised. Our racks held quite a few large, sealed ration packs and every so often we had to take one down and open it to see if the food inside had been contaminated. You'd think this would be impossible, with the tins being sealed but every time I opened one up there'd be weevils crawling all over the place. How they got there I've no idea but there they were anyway. A lot of the food inside the packs was double sealed with thick silver foil and there was plenty of unsoiled grub that was perfectly edible. The policy at the time was to change all the ration packs for fresh ones and distribute all the uncontaminated food to outlying villages. It was warmly welcomed wherever we went. I'm ashamed to admit that I developed a taste for the chocolate bars in these packs and kept a couple back for myself on these occasions. I tried to ease my guilt by sharing some with the lads but the only thanks I got was a spluttered, "Jesus, Taff, this stuff tastes fucking foul!"
I could only think they'd forgotten to brush the weevils off first!

CHAPTER 15

MORE GREEN STUFF

About twelve of us were roped in for a bit of jungle training one sunny day and again, I was more than happy to be included. At the end of the day I wished they'd left me behind!

We entered the jungle in single file and made our way through the undergrowth towards the main area of forest. I was at the back of the file with Jim, one of the Regiment corporals who was giving me a few pointers about what could and could not be eaten and what to do if I was bitten by a snake! I wasn't keen on that bit but at least the previous method of dealing with snake bite had been discarded and this came as a great relief to me.

I'd been shown the snake bite kits when I arrived on the squadron and they were terrifying. They were just small, hollow containers and inside, if memory serves correct, was a sachet of charcoal grains and a tiny scalpel. The instructions were quite simple. If bitten by a snake, make two deep incisions either side of the bite with the scalpel and sprinkle the charcoal on top of the wound. Luckily someone realised that this would probably cause more damage than the snake and God help you if you got bit anywhere near an artery. Thoughts of an over eager gunner treating any bite I happened to get were not pleasant at all.

Having binned the kits we now looked for the new method to be revealed. Bound to be much better and carefully vetted by the medical profession we thought.

"If you get bitten go straight to sick quarters without touching the bite," came the first part of the lesson.

"What if we're out in the wilds and nowhere near sick quarters?" came a pretty sensible query.

"Look, just keep your fucking mouth shut and let me finish, alright?" went the answer.

"Try and get hold of the snake that bit you to allow the doc to identify which anti-venom to use," continued the lesson.

Long, stunned silence until...

"So, lemme get this straight. I get bitten in the bollocks by a fucking great King Cobra and the first thing I do is chase it through the jungle so it can have another go at me. Is this what you're saying?"

Well done Smudge, tell it like it is!

"No, that's not what I'm saying," seethed our snake man, "If you can identify the snake then that's okay. What I'm saying is, if you mis-identify the snake and they give you the wrong anti-venom then you're going to be in a worse fucking state than you were before."

"But aren't we supposed to keep our heart rates down so as not to pump the venom around any quicker than necessary. I'm only guessing here but wouldn't chasing a poisonous snake through the undergrowth make your heart beat like a fucking drum?"

I was left none the wiser after the session and carried an even bigger fear of snakes around with me for the rest of the tour. I can't remember what Jim told me about snake bites but I do remember a very good bit of advice he gave me about leeches.

Just as we were about to enter the jungle forest he grabbed hold of my shoulders and turned me around to face him, away from the rest of the patrol.

"Just keep looking at me, Taff," he said, "and count to thirty."

Well, okay. He must have a reason I thought and did as I was told. Then he turned me around and said, "Now go and find your mates."

I thought he was losing it. How could you possibly lose twelve men in thirty seconds? The simple truth was that you could. Very easily. I couldn't see or hear a thing. I had no idea where they'd gone. I couldn't hear anything apart from the various birds and insects chirping away. It was really un-nerving but showed just how easy it was to get lost in the jungle and it was a sobering thought.

"That's your first priority," said Jim. "Never lose sight of the others because you'll never find them again. Now here's another little tip. When we catch up with them we'll hang about at the back. All the leeches will drop on those silly bastards at the front and with any luck we might end up with only one or two on us."

Now, I didn't even want one of the repulsive little buggers landing on me because they were hideous, blood sucking creatures that gave me the creeps but I made on that I wasn't worried either way.

THIS LEECH HAS ENJOYED A BIT OF A SUCK ALREADY. WHEN THEY LATCH ON TO YOU INITIALLY THEY'RE TINY LITTLE THINGS WITH A BIG APPETITE!

We carried on through the jungle to our destination which was a small village where our transport was waiting to take us back to camp. I'd already picked up one leech which somehow dropped out of the trees and managed to latch on to the tip of my little finger. Usually you didn't feel them clamping on to you but I just felt a slight tug as this thing managed to find a hold. It didn't do to pull them off because the sucker could detach and be left in your skin to fester. We had little containers of a liquid that could be poured over them which worked okay but the favoured method was to touch a lighted cigarette end to the tail of the Leech, which made them withdraw very quickly.

When we came out of the jungle we were met with a sight that makes me shudder even now. Everyone was stood about in various states of undress removing Leeches from each other. I could see blood trickling down naked torsos and huge, engorged leeches being burned off every part of the body. They even got into the boot lace eyes to feast on feet. In its way it was quite funny.

"What the fuck are you laughing at," I was snarled at by our leader (who seemed to have the biggest share of Leeches). "Get your shirt and trousers off and make sure you're clear."

Apart from one that had got inside my boot and the one on my finger I was leech free! The rest of the boys were quite disappointed and made threats to chuck a couple down my shirt to even things up a bit. I think I moved a bit too quick for them though.

One bonus for me that day was catching sight of a huge tree lizard scampering up a tree as we passed. It was a massive thing and I wouldn't have been so happy had it been scampering *down* the tree but it wasn't and I was delighted. After all, what's the point of being able to tell jungle stories if you haven't been threatened by dangerous creatures lurking behind every tree!

CHAPTER 16

GLAMOUR BOYS

I hadn't long been on duty and was enjoying an early morning cuppa with Sgt Jock Mercer in our little haven of peace and quiet when I heard a voice shouting outside. We both ambled to the window for a nose and saw one of the regiment sergeants going from office to office in a big hurry. One or two gunners dashed out, heading somewhere in great haste and suddenly he was heading for our stores.

"Jock, can you spare young Taff here? Something's up and the CO wants about six of us on the hurry up," he asked.

"I don't see why not, Harry" said Jock with a hint of exasperation, "He's never fucking here anyway!"

"Thanks mate," said Harry, "Taff, go and get your greens on. Full webbing and pick up your SMG from the Armoury. Back here quick as you can for transport to the airfield"

I didn't stop to ask questions. I was convinced we were off on another helicopter demonstration exercise and looked forward to another trip to Kuala Lumpur.

The Land Rover screeched to a halt on the airfield, where a Huey was sat with its rotors whining into life. The CO was there with three men in civvies. I was a bit puzzled by this but didn't give it much thought as we all clambered out and were bundled into the Huey with undue haste. We'd no sooner settled than it took off and soared off in a big, wide, banking turn – straight back to where we'd just left! It hovered about five feet up and we were instructed to jump out one at a time. The CO was waiting and I saw one of the civilians alongside him with a camera. We jumped out as told and stood around in a bemused state. The CO was in deep conference with the cameraman and, finally, he came across to us and explained what was going on.

"It's a publicity exercise lads," he said, "you're going to be in the papers back home. Nice photograph of you jumping out of the helicopter and a bit of a write up."

Well, this sounded good. All the girls in the village getting a look at me in action. Be letters arriving by the sackful, asking for a date when I got back home. My rosy thoughts were interrupted by the CO.

"We just need to do it one more time for the photographer. You were too low and too quick for him just then so we'll get the pilot to hover a little bit higher and if you could just try and jump out slowly, that might help!"

That was a real gem of an instruction and all credit to the CO for keeping a straight face. The rest of us looked at each other because we just knew that in a short space of time we were going to be subjected to some grief. It was bad enough the first time. The ground was rock hard and it jarred quite a lot when we hit it from five feet up so God knows what sort of pain it was going to inflict this time around.

*NICK 'STREAKY' BACON ENCOURAGING ME TO JUMP WITH
A PROD FROM HIS RIFLE BARREL*

Around we went again and conversation in the cabin of the Huey wasn't what I'd call of the heroic kind.

"Fucking Hell, this isn't going to go well is it," was one sentiment. It was too late now though. When it came to jumping out I sat on the edge of the cabin with one foot on the landing skid making absolutely sure the photographer was ready before I jumped. I didn't think I'd be in a fit state to do it a third time. At the end of it all the CO was all smiles, shaking hands with the civilians before taking them back to the officer's mess for lunch. The rest of us limped back to the Land Rover with various twisted ankles and strains in different areas but thankfully, nothing broken.

"That didn't take long, Taff," said Jock Mercer when I got back to stores. I told him the story of woe and made sure to add an extra bit of zest to my limp but it didn't impress him at all.

"Serves you right for going off playing silly buggers," he sympathised, "now go and make the fucking tea!"
I just hoped that bit didn't get in the papers!

Just to complete the story, the newsmen wanted a shot of some of the lads in dense jungle. As we were in the middle of Butterworth Airfield, jungle was in short supply. In fact, it was more like a desert. However, like an oasis there was one tiny clump of bushes nearby, with a pathetic, limp looking little palm tree in the middle. The CO was a man of initiative though and put two of the lads in amongst the bushes, kneeling down. He then got two of the others to bend this palm tree over until the fronds were hanging over the jungle warriors. When the photos came out it looked for all the world as though they were entangled in the thickest jungle Malaya had to offer!

My photo went in the South Wales Echo and half the village stuck a copy through Mum and Dad's letterbox. Nick, who was behind me in the photo, was a Canadian and I've no idea where his photo went. Rocky Mountains Gazette or something similar I expect.

CHAPTER 17

ALL CREATURES, GREAT AND SMALL

Dogs were everywhere on the camp. The majority were strays of differing varieties and some of them were in a terrible condition. Half starved, feral animals that were subjected to regular 'culling.' This was carried out by shooting any dog that could be found without an identification bracelet to show they'd been suitably inoculated against disease. It wasn't a pleasant thing to watch as the culling was carried out around the camp and a lot of the squadrons would 'adopt' a dog to prevent it being shot.

1 Squadron was no exception but they opted for a monstrous beast of a dog that looked as though it could have been fathered by a Bengal tiger! It was part Alsatian, part Pit Bull and all aggro. He was named 'Tunku' and roamed about the place as if he owned it. He came into my life as I was stood in stores looking out of the window at the CO inspecting a squad of gunners one day. As he moved down the first line, Tunku suddenly appeared and started walking along the line with him. The CO tried to shoo him away but Tunku was having none of

it. Finally losing his patience the CO told one of his sergeants to get rid of the dog until the parade was over and that's when I became personally involved.

"Price, come and get this dog and shut him in the stores with you until we've finished out here," shouted the sergeant who'd been tasked with getting rid of the dog. Why he chose me I don't know because I'd always been wary of dogs and I didn't really relish the idea of imprisoning Tunku in the same room as me. However, an order's an order so out I went. I walked up to the dog and tried the soft approach with a few, "Here, Tunku, here boy," requests but he just looked at me with his head cocked to one side and a look of puzzlement in his eyes.

"For Christ's sake, grab him by the collar," I was ordered. I moved forward with my hand outstretched and this immediately drew a low growl and a slow shift into attack mode. I snatched my hand back and took a pace backwards. I tried once more and this time I received a very loud bark for my troubles. I stepped back a bit further this time.

"Doesn't want to go, sir," I said to the CO, who was getting visibly annoyed by this time. Then a very brave man in the form of our flight sergeant stormed over, grabbed Tunku by the collar and started dragging him off towards stores. There was a lot of wheezing and struggling going on but eventually he chucked the dog inside and shut the door on him.

"Keep him there until we've finished out here," he told me, "Give him a bowl of water and some hard tack biscuits to keep him quiet."

Fair enough. I put my hand on the door and started to turn the handle – all Hell erupted from the other side – I took my hand off the handle and peered through the window. The dog jumped at the window as though he'd like to tear me limb from limb.

"What the *fuck* is going on?" came a quiet voice behind me.

"Dog won't let me in, Flight," I replied nervously.

"For fucks sake, stay outside then. Open the door and let him out when we've all gone," he snarled.

And that's what I did. As soon as the area was clear I threw open the door and flattened myself against the wall whilst this hound from Hell erupted from within and charged off looking for something to murder. I'm still nervous of dogs to this day and is it any wonder...?

I'd been sent to pick up some gear from main stores one afternoon and decided I'd take the bike that was parked outside, leaning against a palm tree. It was used by all the flight for various small errands and saved the legs a bit of exercise. I wasn't paying attention as I approached the bike but a shout came from outside one of the offices opposite.

"You taking that bike somewhere, Taff?" asked one of the gunners.

"Just popping over to main stores, George," I replied.

"Fair enough mate. Are you taking the snake as well?" This, naturally, brought me to a standstill and I looked frantically around for a deadly reptile heading my way.

"What snake?" I shouted

"The one wrapped around the handlebars," came the answer. He wasn't joking either and there it was, curled peacefully over the handlebars enjoying a nap in the sun. I'd no idea what sort of snake it was but I'd decided that every snake in Malaya was deadly poisonous as far as I was concerned and, as such, I kept well away from this thing. George and a couple of other gunners ambled over for a look and decided that it couldn't be left where it was. A brush was produced and the snake was unceremoniously hooked off the bike and clouted around the head. Why they did this I don't know because the snake went from peaceful doze mode to maddened, rearing up, hissing mode in half a second flat. I ran back into stores and the rest of the heroes dispersed with disdainful haste. I kept an eye on it from out of the window and after a few darting moves in differing directions it slithered off into the grass looking just about as pissed off as a snake with a sore head could look. I put off my trip to main stores and found some compelling task that kept me inside for most of the day!

Mosquitoes were the bane of our life out in the Far East and I was destined to be given my first lesson about them by gunners from 1 LAA Squadron. It happened long before I joined the regiment, on the first day of my arrival at Butterworth. A bed couldn't be found for me in the airmen's blocks and I was directed to the RAF Regiment block until I could be permanently billeted. I was brand new. A 'Moonie' as every sun burned veteran called those who were straight out from the UK, looking startlingly white with their sun starved bodies.

 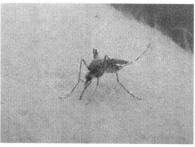

ONLY FEMALE MOSQUITOES SUCK BLOOD. MALES FEED ON THE NECTAR OF FLOWERS. NOT UNLIKE HUMANS REALLY!

There was a mosquito net rolled up at the head of my bed and I wasn't sure what the situation was regarding them. I made the mistake of asking the lads in the billet if I needed a net or were they just for a particular season of the year. Now this was a temptation too far for these gunners. Here was not only a Moonie but a penguin to boot and the chance for a bit of sport far outweighed their concern for a fellow human being.

"Nah, mate. You don't need those fucking things. Mosquitoes won't bother you in billets like this," I was told.

I woke up at about 0600 bitten half to death by what felt like a couple of squadrons of mosquitoes. My pale white body and face were covered in itchy blotches and I looked like something out of a contagious diseases ward! I looked across at my regiment room mates only to see them half hidden by firmly tucked in mosquito nets. It was a lesson I could have done without to be honest but at least it left me with no illusions about bloody rock apes. When I moved over to the airmen's billet I told everyone what a bunch of bastards they were! It wasn't a good start to my relationship with the Royal Air Force Regiment.

Mosquitoes aside we also had big, black, flying beetles to contend with. They had shells that were practically armour plated and every so often one of them would stray off course and fly into the billet. This usually resulted in people diving under beds or getting outside as fast as possible because every room had a big fan in the middle of the ceiling, whirring around to cool us down. Inevitably the beetle would scoot around in a frenzy, looking for a way out and, also inevitably, it would fly into the fan. There'd be a big clatter and the body of the beetle would be propelled like a bullet out of its circle and smack into whatever came into its path first. It could be a bed or a cupboard or, if you were desperately unlucky, it could be human flesh. Bits of shell flew about like shrapnel and it was a state of chaos until the beetle lay splattered where it lay. Naturally, sport could also be made of this situation. At the first sign of a beetle the last man heading for the door would find it slammed in his face and held shut in the hope he'd get zapped. Not very funny when you look back on it but hilarious at the time!

ARMOURED RHINOSCEROUS BEETLE

Chit Chats were small lizards that inhabited every billet and when I first saw them I was somewhat alarmed to see them scuttling across the ceiling in search of food. I soon learned that they were friends though, getting rid of flies and insects. I was laying on my bed on one occasion and felt a little plop on my stomach. I looked down to find a Chit Chat stood there looking at me in a bemused way. He'd lost his grip on the ceiling but found a safe landing. They were friendly little creatures though and we enjoyed their amiable company.

A FRIENDLY CHIT-CHAT

CHAPTER 18

BLESSED ARE THEY...

I was due to celebrate my 21st birthday on the 21st August 1966 but a week before that memorable occasion I was pencilled in for my first free fall parachute descent at Bayan Lepas Airfield. It was a nervous sort of a time for me and before the day was over I found out that I had every reason to be nervous!

I'd come to rely on the static line opening my parachute for me and the thought that the whole circus would now be in my hands entirely wasn't a comforting one. I'd worked out a hundred things that could go wrong and they exceeded things that could go right by a very long stretch! A couple of my mates opted to come over to watch and we decided to spend the night before in the Hong Kong Bar, Penang. This was a hugely popular bar with servicemen and the owners were very friendly towards us. We had a whale of a time and, at the end of a long evening asked if the three of us could stay overnight to save going all the way back to Butterworth. This was readily agreed but, as it wasn't a hotel, we'd just have to sit slumped over a table to get our sleep. We'd all slept in worse places so gladly accepted the offer.

The following morning I awoke at first light and ambled over to the window for an early breakfast of two cigarettes! It was a grey sort of day and had that horrible, early morning reality feel about it. Gone were the bright lights and laughter of the night before, to be replaced by the ominous silence of an oriental dawn. I felt like death on a winter's morning, was unwashed, unshaven and my overwhelming thought was that the very last thing in the world I wanted to do was to go and step out of an aeroplane in a couple of hours time!

"*Jesus*, Robert. You look fucking awful! Be a kindness if you fell to your death really!" greeted Bob Milligan when I turned up at the airfield. As words of encouragement go these didn't quite afford the level of comfort I craved but I had to make do with them anyway. I started to get kitted up and Bob talked me through the procedures as my parachute was buckled on.

As per normal everything was removed from my flying suit first off. Cigarettes, lighter, loose change – anything that could possibly present a hazard in the air. I kept looking at the 'D' ring, knowing it was now 'live' and not just a 'dummy.' I practiced reaching for it with my eyes closed just to make sure I knew exactly where it was. I didn't fancy the idea of forgetting where it was while I was busy plummeting out of the sky at 120 mph!

Bob then told me he wouldn't be acting as my dispatcher this time and my stomach lurched even lower. He'd dispatched me for all my jumps up to then and I really wanted him with me this time. He might have been a tough taskmaster but he was an absolute expert when it came to parachuting and we all felt safe with him in the aircraft with us. My dismay must have shown on my face because he was quick to re-assure me that I'd be in very safe hands. My dispatcher was to be Captain Mike Seeger, Royal Marines and this cheered me up a bit because you didn't come across too many marine captains who were incompetent!

He was quite a tall, imposing man who gave me a warm smile as he shook my hand. He shook it again after the jump but that was more of a congratulatory handshake – a sort of well done for still being in one piece sort of handshake…!

As I was getting ready to walk down to the aircraft one of my mates took the time to tell me that it was the 13th of the month and this took me by surprise as well. It's not that I was superstitious but it was an added worry to chuck in with all the other worries sat in my head.

"Come on then, Robert. Let's get you out to the Cessna," said Bob Milligan and we started out for the short walk to the aeroplane.

"Hang on fellas," came a shout from behind us. "I've just had the tower on. There's a passenger aircraft due in about half an hour. They want us to abort until it's down."

Oh, fucking *hell*. That was just about the last straw. If I hadn't been a nervous wreck before I certainly was now.

I was eased into a deck chair, still fully harnessed up for the jump. I took my helmet off and begged a fag off one of the boys. Then I just sat there, staring out at the airfield. I didn't want to talk to anyone and it was just about the longest half hour I've spent in my entire life! Let's just say I've had more tranquil moments in my life and leave it at that.

Eventually the passenger aircraft landed and we were given clearance to carry on. Back out to the Cessna we went and Captain Seeger carried out a pre flight check on my equipment before climbing into the back of the aircraft. Just to explain a bit about jumping from a Cessna, there was room for two parachutists in the back and one sat on the floor (passenger side). This entailed the side door being removed to allow us to climb out when the time came. I was to be first out and therefore took my seat on the floor directly in front of Captain Seeger. There was a strap located on the door frame for me to hang on to and this was all there was to stop me falling out! When it came to the jump I'd climb out and put one foot on the wheel and one on a step on the wheel strut whilst putting both hands on the wing strut, facing forward.

Captain Seeger making final equipment checks before first free fall

The recommended height for a first free fall at the time was 3,000ft but due to cloud conditions we had to settle for 2,700ft. This was a bit unsettling because extra height was extra time to react if anything went wrong.

We taxied out and lined up for the take off run, the engine noise very loud in the open cabin. The Cessna moved forward slowly and quickly gathered speed before lifting into the air. Before my first jump I'd been advised not to look down but the slowly receding ground held a sort of fascination for me and I couldn't take my eyes off it as it dropped away far below. Then we were running in to the exit point and Captain Seeger put his hand on my shoulder as he leaned forward to shout to the pilot.

"Brakes on, throttles off."

This should have resulted in the brakes locking the wheels to give me a firm base for my right foot and the engine easing back to idling speed to slow us down for the jump. I suppose getting one out of two right wasn't too bad in the circumstances!

"Okay, out you go," shouted my dispatcher and I leaned out to put my right foot on the wheel. When I put my weight on it the wheel spun around and my foot shot off into mid-air. I was left scrabbling around like a fly in a spider's web.

"What the Hell are you doing," yelled Captain Seeger.

"The wheels aren't locked," I screamed back and he quickly got the message to the pilot. I was then able to get into position ready for the jump. Usually there'd be a little pause before the command to jump but, what with all the drama with the wheel, we'd drifted on past the exit point. I'd barely got my right hand on the wing strut when...

"GO!"

It was all a bit frantic but at least it didn't give me too much time to dwell on things and I was falling away from the Cessna before I was fully aware of my surroundings. I started my count.

"One thousand." *look down and locate 'D' ring.* "Two thousand." *Bring right hand across and grab 'D' ring whilst bringing left hand across in front of helmet to maintain stability.* "Three thousand." *Pull 'D' ring out of its housing and throw both arms back out to maintain the spread-eagle falling position.* It went like clockwork, right up until the time the 'D' ring got stuck after moving just a couple of inches!

There are times in life when things flash through your mind at a great rate of knots and this was one of mine. My thought process took in several things all at once and seemed to merge into one in a split second. Oddly, my first thought was that I'd pulled the 'D' ring out far enough to deploy the canopy and I made no attempt to pull it further. Then, almost simultaneously, I thought I'd better not leave it there and gave it another good, hard pull. This time it came away and my canopy snaked out above me. For the first time ever I actually had my head thrown back far enough to see it streaming out above me but again, this didn't have the desired effect of offering the comfort it should have. When the 'D' ring stuck I'd already thrown my left arm out in anticipation of the right arm lining up with it to keep myself in a stable position. That little manoeuvre put me into a spin and as I watched the canopy streaming out I could plainly see it was spinning in sympathy!

Suddenly, I was snatched upright in the usual controlled violence of a parachute cracking open overhead. I tried to look up to check my canopy only to find that the lines had twisted behind my back forcing me into a slightly bent, face down position. I had the most wonderful view of Bayan Lepas Airfield below me but, to be honest, I wasn't really in a sight seeing frame of mind at the time. Then, very slowly, the earth began to spin around as the rigging lines unwound themselves before finally settling where they should be settled. I checked the canopy – all deployed - no problems. I checked the ground, which now looked to be a lot closer than it should have been. I found out later that my planned three second free fall drop lasted almost double the time!

I was nowhere near the drop zone and looked set for a landing in a big field across the other side of the airfield. It looked like it was ploughed and it looked like it might make for a bit of a rough landing but by then I just didn't care. All I wanted was to get my feet on solid ground and find someone whose shoulder I could cry on!

I smacked into the ground with the usual amount of grunting and thumping – and just lay where I'd fallen. I was, I suppose, in a state of shock because I'd no idea how long I lay there trying to go through it all again and make sense out of what'd just happened. I knew it hadn't gone to plan but it all happened so fast I wasn't able to comprehend quite what had taken place and what hadn't. I managed to roll over and unbuckle my harness but my hands were shaking a bit too much for me to unclip my helmet. I looked towards the clubhouse and saw someone running in my direction. Then I heard a tractor approaching. It was a Malay farmer, little conical sun hat shading his eyes.

"You jump from aeroplane?" he asked.

"Yes," was all I managed to croak. He looked at me for what seemed like a long time, smiled and drove off. I've no idea what that smile meant. Judge for yourselves.

By then, the running figure had materialised into Ron Taylor and he came up to me with a worried look and a, "You alright, Taff?" on his lips.

"Not really Ron. Did you bring your fags?"

"Yeah," he said, dragging a packet out of his pocket. I was in desperate need and marked Ron down as a prince among men. I stuck it between my trembling lips whilst he searched for a light.

"Ah, left my lighter behind didn't I," he laughed. I've spoken to Ron on several occasions over the years and he had his own traumas in the air, not least being knocked out by a loose altimeter on his reserve 'chute but I honestly believe that he never came closer to dying than at that brief moment in time in 1966!

Ron helped me carry my gear back and Captain Seeger was waiting to speak to me.

"I thought you were going to leave that 'D' ring where it was for one horrible moment," he said.

"I gave it some thought, sir" I said, "The 'chute was opening anyway wasn't it?"

"No, it bloody wasn't," he replied and that was probably the first time I realised how close I'd come to a bit of real drama.

When I entered the jump in my log book I put down, 'Bad pull, twists, bad landing.' Bob Milligan went to sign it as authorising officer and said, "What d'you mean bad landing? You fucking walked away from it didn't you and if you can do that then it's a good landing."

God bless you, Bob Milligan, for not letting me get overly dramatic.

CHAPTER 19

A SPELL AT CHINA ROCK

The light anti aircraft practice range known as China Rock lies off the coast of Johore near Singapore. It was a quiet little backwater but every so often noisy buggers used to descend on it with 40/70 Bofors guns and make life a living hell for anybody or anything living nearby! This time it was to be 1 LAA and one of the Singapore based regiment squadrons. Not to mention one or two bemused penguins.

My job on this exercise was to load up everything we'd need for a fortnight under canvas and set up a stores tent on arrival. I'd be covering the first part of the exercise and Jock Mercer would travel down to take over for the second part. I was to travel down as part of a road convoy from Butterworth to Singapore, a journey of approximately 400 miles. This sounded good to me. Sit alongside the driver in the cab of the three tonner, feet on the dashboard and smoking the odd cheroot whilst enjoying the passing scenery.

On the day the convoy left I went to jump in the cab only to find Taff Hopton sat in the passenger seat. He was to act as relief driver on the way down. Bill was in the driver's seat.

"Where am I supposed to sit?" I asked politely.

"Well, you could sit on the fucking bumper but you'll probably find it's a bit more comfortable in the back," I was told sarcastically.

"But the back's full of gear," I objected.

"Tough. It's either that or fucking walk…"

'WE'VE GOT OURSELVES A CONVOY'
ON THE ROAD TO SINGAPORE

I spent the entire journey stuck in the back of that truck, jammed in between tents and numerous other objects of an uncomfortable nature. All I had for company was my SMG. Due to the ongoing threat from Indonesia we were all armed and live ammunition was being carried in the convoy. I just hoped I could enjoy a smoke without blowing us up!

We stopped overnight just outside kuala Lumpur and slept in the trucks. A large fire was lit to ward off the mosquitoes and a washroom was provided for us a short walk from the vehicles. I was stood by the fire late on in the evening and Frank Sylvester was alongside me enjoying a quiet moment. One of the lads, Tom, came out of the washroom and started making his way towards us when he suddenly collapsed and lay still.

Frank grabbed me by the arm and said, "Go and get the Medic Taff, quickly."

"That's Tom, sir," I told him, "He *is* the medic!"

"For fuck's sake," he managed to get out before dashing off to administer help and succour to our fallen comrade. Happily, Tom was soon on his feet and declaring himself fit to carry on. It was a worrying moment though.

A QUICK BREAK AT KUALA LUMPUR

I climbed into the back of my luxury accommodation and made myself as comfortable as possible on top of a couple of folded tents. Then the mosquitoes came. Thousands of them it seemed and all intent on eating me alive. I couldn't see them in the dark but I could plainly hear the little buzzing sound as they zeroed in around my head. It was a maddening noise. It would start with a quiet buzz which increased rapidly until suddenly cutting out. A bit like '*zzzzzzzzzzt!*' It only stopped when it landed on you and stuck its needle sharp sucker into your skin. I pulled out a mosquito net and dragged it right over me like a shroud. I spent about an hour of maddening torment before giving up and I wasn't the only one who gave up on sleep either. I joined a small group of gunners who'd also sought sanctuary from the blood sucking insects and we huddled around the fire in miserable exhaustion, sharing a fag and a good old British serviceman's moan.

We eventually arrived in Singapore where we boarded LCT (Landing Craft Tank) Arromanches for the final leg of the journey to China Rock. The LCTs weren't designed for comfort and again, we were left to find whatever bit of exposed deck afforded some measure of relief for our aching bones. As we were leaving Singapore harbour

LCT 'ARDENNES' SISTER SHIP TO LCT ARROMANCHES

we were all dragged to our feet, made to tidy ourselves up and form line for leaving harbour. We had one or two waves from the docks crowd but nobody seemed remotely interested in our departure. All very disappointing but we were told it was custom for troops to line up as a ship was leaving harbour so line up we did. It was a long journey by sea to China Rock but it was pleasantly cool on the deck and I even managed a bit of much needed sleep stretched out on a canvas covered bit of freight. Some five hours later we beached at China Rock.

The three tonners drove off the ramp but we were told to just get into the water and wade ashore. It only came up to just above our jungle boots thankfully and it only took a minute or two to reach the beach, where a very excited young officer was dashing about asking if anybody had taken any photos. It seems he was at the front of the wading line of men and desperately wanted a heroic picture to send home. When everybody shook their heads he ordered us back to the landing craft to do it all again. This time he made sure somebody was taking photos!

I set up shop in my stores tent and chalked '1 SQUADRON STORES' on the top. It was just my way of marking my territory! The rest of the day was spent unloading all the gear and settling in for the coming busy days. Everything was under canvas but at least there was ice available to ensure our supply of beer was nicely chilled for the evenings and that went down very well. There was little in the way of entertainment other than a portable cinema screen and projector. I can only remember one of the films, 'Guns at Batasi,' with Richard Attenborough shouting his way through his role as a company sergeant major. I had good reason to remember it as well...

Due to the ongoing war with Indonesia, armed guards patrolled the camp throughout the night and I had to take my turn with everyone else. Again I found myself with a rifle instead of my SMG. I don't know why they gave it to me to be honest. On the night the film was shown I was on guard duty, doing my rounds. When the film started I couldn't resist lurking beside one of the tents to watch a bit before moving on but I became engrossed and probably stayed a bit longer than was wise.

"What the fuck d'you think you're doing?" came a quiet voice beside my ear. Frank Sylvester had spotted me and zeroed in for a bollocking.

"Just stopped for a breather, sir," I said in desperation.

"Well it was a fucking long breather. Now fuck off and do what you're supposed to be doing," he suggested. I had no option other than to sling my rifle back on my shoulder and stride off with a look of intense aggression on my face!

Night guards were a bit of a drag. As I remember two of us would patrol the camp for two hours then go back to the guard tent for a couple of hours sleep whilst two more went out. We'd go our separate ways to circle the camp and generally meet up as we crossed over. Sometimes we'd have a quick natter and a smoke before moving on which broke the monotony a bit.

On the first day of the exercise a Meteor aircraft towing a sleeve target flew overhead and the guns, lined up at the top of the beach, opened up with a thunderous roar. The noise was incredible. Like being in the middle of a prolonged, violent thunderstorm. A crate of beer was on offer to the first gun crew to hit the target and naturally, competition was fierce. I'd gone down to watch the shoot and was just itching to have a go myself. I'd already asked about this and been given a favourable, if guarded, answer. No chance on the first day but come back the following day. If the lads on the gun were prepared to give up their break time to show me the ropes then I'd be allowed to have a shoot.

The following day I went down to the gun line and paid attention to the firing sequence as I watched the lads in action. Without going into too much detail there was a gun safety officer stood behind each gun who held a firing inhibitor. This inhibitor prevented the gun being fired until he'd lifted the firing inhibits. His job was to ensure the target was being tracked by the No3 (Gun Layer) and that the towing aircraft had passed safely overhead before enabling the gun to fire. It all seemed straightforward to me!

BOFORS 40/70 IN ACTION AT CHINA ROCK

The lads on the gun were only too happy to give me a bit of training and I was plonked into the layer's seat for my instruction.

"Use the foot pedal to fire, Taff and elevate the barrel by winding the Azimuth handle. As soon as you pick up the target in your sights shout, 'ON,' to let us know you're tracking it. Keep tracking it until you hear the shout, 'SAFE TO SHOOT' followed by 'FIRE.' As soon as you hear that, start shooting. Clear enough?"

"Yeah, I think so," I said.

"Don't just fucking *think* so. Are you clear on it or not?"

"Perhaps just one more run through then, just to make sure." I replied. We went through it all about three more times until I was repeating it out loud.

"Pick up target – shout 'ON' - wind handle – keep sights on target – wait for safe to shoot and the fire command – press foot pedal to shoot."

The boss was informed that I was now a fully trained Bofors gunner and I duly took my place for the next live shoot. Looking back I think I was probably a bit too hyped up and way too eager to blast away with this big gun because the shoot didn't go well at all!

'IT'S QUITE SIMPLE. AIM – SHOUT – BANG! EVEN A PENGUIN CAN DO IT.'

I picked up the target early on and my heart leapt with excitement. I thought it would have been the hardest part but there it was, sat right in the middle of my sights. I began winding the handle to keep track of it and the barrel slowly lifted as it drew closer. It kept on drawing closer - and closer still. I heard the other guns begin firing and I was in a frenzy of impatience. I even shouted to the lads behind me that I could see the target but they didn't respond. Then it was too late. The target was gone and so was my chance of ever firing a Bofors gun again. I was more than a little annoyed and when the drill was over I climbed out of the layer's seat and spoke my piece.

"Why didn't I get the safe to shoot shout? I tracked that sleeve right from the start," I argued. The Boss had come up by then and he seemed to be holding back a bit of pent up rage.

"Did I just hear you say you picked up the target straight off," he said quietly. I'd rather he shouted to be honest. When they said something like that quietly it usually meant the wrath of God was about to descend on someone.

"Yes, sir," I replied, equally quietly, for I was beginning to realise that the fault may *just* lay somewhere other than at his doorstep.

"Well why didn't you shout 'on' to let us know you were tracking it?"

Ah! Yes. Light dawned and heavenly choirs broke into song.

"Oh, fuck it! Sorry, sir. I completely forgot. Can I have another go? I won't forget this time."

In all fairness he took a good split second before saying no and sloping off in a dejected manner. I was a bit puzzled because it didn't seem such a big deal to me. Saved them the cost of a few shells hadn't I? It's taken until now to find out why it was such a big deal.

Apparently it meant that the detachment would have missed a firing run caused by incorrect drills, resulting in one mega pissed off No1 who was going to get a very uncomfortable interview with the flight commander. In turn, the flight commander would have received similar treatment from the CO. Oh, well. Into every life a little rain must fall I suppose.

Making a complete hash of firing the Bofors aside, I enjoyed my stay at China Rock although it wasn't always a laugh a minute. Someone had been found with a case of 'crabs,' tiny little lice that fed exclusively on blood (why was everything intent on sucking the blood out of us out there?). They were usually to be found burrowing under the pubic hairs and every one of us, from the CO down, were subjected to an intimate inspection by our medic. One at a time we entered his tent and were subjected to a thorough check. It was at this point that I thanked all the gods I hadn't chosen to be a medic!

On the day I was due to leave China Rock I'd packed all my kit, handed over my bed and was looking forward to a hot shower and a cold beer in Singapore before flying back to Butterworth the following day. Then I was told I'd have to stay another day until Jock Mercer arrived and I watched enviously as all the boys who were returning to Singapore boarded the waiting LCT. I stood on the beach watching it sail slowly away, ignoring the two fingered farewell waves and shouted obscenities floating across the water.

"I've got nowhere to sleep tonight, Sarge," I told one of the NCOs plaintively.

"No bother at all, Taff," he replied. "You can kip down in the guard tent. Might as well give one of the lads a break and do a guard duty as well while you're at it."

Well, thank you very fucking much indeed. Just what I need. I dumped all my kit in the tent and settled in for another tiring night duty. It was to prove an interesting night though. For all the wrong reasons.

I was getting ready to go out for my first couple of hours when I noticed the other guard who was paired up with me fixing his bayonet on the end of his rifle! I was a bit alarmed by this but made a bit of a joke about it to ease the tension. He didn't laugh. He just said, "The bastards won't get me without a fight, Taff," and went out into the night, leaving me a very worried man. The guard commander had a quiet word with me and told me not to worry. It was just a bit of a thing he had, I was told. Apparently he always fixed bayonets when on guard duty. I made a point of calling out to him well in advance of us passing each other on our rounds. I wanted to make absolutely certain he didn't mistake me for an Indonesian commando or something!

On my second stint of the night I was just about all in. I'd had no sleep all day and very little the previous night after a lengthy 'Farewell to the Rock' drinking session. I was on the beach section of the round and this was the bit I liked least. It was pitch black for a start and totally deserted. The gentle slap of the waves breaking on the shore and the assorted chirpings of night time insects didn't help my fatigue much either. In fact they were lulling me into a state of lethargy. Then I spotted a figure moving on the beach and this gave me a bit of a jolt because it was the middle of the night and nobody should have been there. I moved a bit closer and called out a challenge. No answer. I took my rifle off my shoulder and called out a bit louder.

Still no answer and, by now, I was getting more than a little jumpy. Then a voice spoke out of the darkness behind me.

"What the fuck're you doing, Taff?" the voice asked. I almost passed out on the spot.

"*Jesus Christ,* Scouse, you fucking idiot. You frightened me to bloody death," I managed to croak. "I think someone's on the beach," I added.

Being braver than me he went forward for a shuftee at the spot I'd indicated. A few seconds later he called back that he'd found my intruder. My 'figure' moving about on the beach was nothing more than a beach marker flag swaying about in the gentle breeze. Mixed emotions came then. Huge relief that I wasn't about to become involved in a life or death struggle with an Indonesian frogman and deep dread that my escapade would be recounted to the whole camp the next day. I lit a cigarette to calm my jangling nerves and offered one to Scouse. Then I asked him if he'd be so kind as to not tell anyone about this little mis-identification of mine. I suppose it was too much to ask of a bloody rock ape really but, to be fair, he didn't tell anyone. He told everyone!

All smiles as we leave China Rock

Guard duty over, I gathered my gear together yet again and prepared to leave China Rock. There were only about six of us leaving and we wouldn't be going back on an LCT this time. Instead a small, open decked motor boat was going to be taking us back to Singapore and this meant being driven to its mooring in a three tonner. The short journey took us along what was just about the roughest dirt track I've ever seen in my life, wending its way through plantations and kampongs. Some of the pot holes were horrendous. It would have been quicker to walk but we weren't overly worried. We were off to Singapore and all its carnal delights!

It wasn't a bad journey back and, eventually we could just see Singapore in the distance. I was lounging about in the back and idly looking out to sea when a massive upheaval of water sprang up a couple of hundred yards off our port side. It was a huge eruption of white water and it frightened the hell out of everyone. Then a periscope appeared, quickly followed by a massive conning tower. Finally, the whole submarine surfaced in what was quite a magnificent sight. It looked like an American submarine but I couldn't be sure. As we watched, white suited sailors began streaming out on to the deck and lining up for entering harbour. It was very impressive. I thought our little motor launch was making good speed but this thing left us for standing as it surged on by. We gave them a friendly wave but they must have taken us for vagrants or something because they didn't wave back! We did look a little on the scruffy side I suppose. Unshaven, sweat stained jungle greens, some with shirts off altogether and all of us lolling about in a very unmilitary fashion. Never mind. Soon be spruced up for a trip down to Singapore.

As we walked in to the transit billet I bumped into a good mate of mine from Butterworth. He'd been posted to Borneo in my absence and was stopping over for one night before heading out the next day.

Fate put us both in the same spot on the one day we were both destined to regret.

Woody was all for a momentous night out to celebrate this meeting and for a fitting way to say cheerio to each other. By the end of the night we were drowning in Tiger beer and looking for something to commemorate this emotional farewell. The idea, when it came, seemed absolutely brilliant.

"Let's gerra tattoo," one of us slurred.

"S'brilliant idea," said the other. Luckily, there were no tattooists on Penang or anywhere else near Butterworth but Singapore was home to many a colourful needle parlour. Why I thought it was a brilliant idea I don't know because my aversion to needles was still with me. Tiger beer however, had a way of lending courage to the inebriated and off we went.

We ended up in a tattoo parlour run by an old Chinese man named Johnny Two Thumbs due to a large, deformed thumb. As the two of us had made our first parachute jumps together I decided that I wanted a parachute wings tattoo at the top of my left arm. I reasoned that this was the only way I was going to get a set of wings on my shoulder as the RAF had so rudely declined to let me earn a proper set! I felt little pain throughout the whole sitting. A few jars of Tiger proved a wonderful anaesthetic!

The following morning I woke up in the transit billet with a massive hangover and the first thing I noticed was a blood stained bandage covering my tattoo. It was really sore as well. It took weeks to heal and I vowed never to get another one as long as I lived. I've managed to keep that vow so far. Woody had gone by the time I woke up but I went to his wedding several years later. I showed him my tattoo and blamed him entirely for me being branded for life.

"It's alright for you, mate," he answered, "Look what I bloody ended up with." He rolled his sleeve up and there, in magnificent technicolour, was a lion standing on a globe of the world holding a Union Flag in its paw. It stretched from his wrist to his shoulder and must have hurt like a bugger while it was healing. It was the only bit of pleasure I got out of the whole experience!

I flew back to Butterworth in another Bristol 'Frightener' and the incessant noise and vibration did wonders for my hangover! When I got back to the billet I had a shower and went straight to bed, where I stayed until the following afternoon. It was one of the very few times I enjoyed doing absolutely nothing at all.

CHAPTER 20

THE FINAL CURTAIN

Back on the squadron life was very peaceful, with half of the lads still away at China Rock and I had little to do other than the usual paperwork and take my turn at making the tea. If I thought it was going to stay that way I was sadly mistaken.

I'd gone out in a Matador for some reason or other. Ginge was driving and we had about three local civilian workers in the back.

MATADOR HEAVY TOWING VEHICLE

We were trundling along steadily and I was quite enjoying the ride when Ginge looked across at me and said, "D'you fancy a laugh? Look at that crowd in the back and see what happens."
I was always glad of a laugh because I didn't get too many of them so I turned around to look at the poor buggers in the back. I thought Ginge was going to make a sudden swerve to chuck them across the truck but that wasn't what he had in mind at all...

It's difficult to recall exactly what happened next but whatever it was, it happened in a split second. I had a brief awareness of forward movement and a loud crashing of broken glass. When full awareness returned I was hanging upside down outside the Matador looking at the front bumper and the front part of a very large tyre! It was total shock and I just hung there trying to make sense out of what had just happened. I could see broken glass on the road and knew I'd gone through the windscreen. I managed to twist my body around and looked back up at the cab where I could make out Ginge's shocked face looking down at me. He must have been just as shocked as me and we just looked at each other for what seemed a long time. Then he said, "What the fuck're you doing out there?" which was quite a puzzling thing to say in the circumstances. He had, after all, been the one who put me out there in the first place and he must have had a fair idea of what I was doing draped over the front of his truck.

I think we both came to our senses at the same time and Ginge moved quickly over to my side of the Matador and grabbed hold of my legs. I started to claw my way back up and, with Ginge's frantic help, managed to get back into the cab. We were both breathing heavily and I began to take stock of my injuries. I couldn't feel any pain and a quick check revealed only a slight nick on my arm that was bleeding slightly. I couldn't believe I'd got away without anything more serious but I soon found out why. The Matador's front screen was in two sections. The bottom half was solid glass but the top part was hinged to allow the top to be open. A bit like a house window. Luckily the top screen on my side was open and, because I'd been turned around looking in the back of the truck, I'd hit it with my shoulder as I flew forward. The glass smashed but the top screen flew up and I went through it without touching the sides! That's what it felt like anyway but my legs had caught on the bottom edge of the screen and stopped me crashing to the ground. I was incredibly lucky and it could have been a lot worse than it actually was. It turned out that Ginge's idea of a laugh was to jam on the brakes, not swerve as I'd anticipated. As we had no safety belts in the truck there was nothing to stop me on my trip outside as it were.

When we got back to the squadron one of the flight lieutenants came up to examine the smashed screen.

"What happened then?" he asked Ginge.

"Well, it was quite funny actually, sir," he said and went on to explain how he'd been forced to make an emergency stop for some non-existent hazard in the road which resulted in my confined space free fall! He got away with it of course but had the grace to apologise to me afterwards. If I could have stopped my hands shaking so much I think I might have strangled him!

In August 1966 the Indonesian Confrontation came to an end and the need for airfield defence was no longer required. In October of 1966 1 LAA received a repatriation order advising that the squadron was to return to the UK in December. It came as a total shock to me and I couldn't quite accept that my time with the RAF Regiment was coming to an end. There was jubilation from those going home of course but those with more than six months of their two and a half year tour left would be transferred to one of the regiment squadrons in Singapore. I spotted a glimmer of light and sought out Squadron Leader Adams.

"What's up, Price?" he asked when I accosted him outside his office one day, "I suppose you'd like to come home with the squadron would you?"

I still had about a year left of my tour and this wasn't exactly what I was after.

"Not really, Sir," I replied, "But what are my chances of going to one of the regiment squadrons in Singapore with the other lads?"

"You want to stay with the RAF Regiment?" he said with considerable surprise. It wasn't often that a request to stay with the RAF Regiment came from a penguin. In fact it was far more common for them to request a move *away* from them! He told me he couldn't authorise that himself but would certainly speak with my stores CO, Squadron Leader Arnold and ask him if it would be possible for a posting to be arranged.

As it turned out, my fate had already been sealed. When the Squadron left I was to be sent to RAF Western Hill, a radar station on top of Penang hill. I'd be billeted with a small RAF unit at Minden Barracks, an army camp occupied by the Royal Green Jackets. To get to the camp at Western Hill every morning meant a trip by road to the Penang Hill Cable railway, a long, slow drag to the top of the hill by cable car and then a further haul by Land Rover through the jungle to the camp.

When I first got sight of it I thought it was a prison camp! It was surrounded by jungle and completely encircled with a high wire fence. I began to think that Squadron Leader Arnold wanted me as far away as possible and in a secure environment for the remainder of my tour!

Things began to wind down as the time for departure came and we found ourselves with long periods of inactivity. This couldn't be allowed of course and various little diversions were dreamed up to keep us focussed. First off was a route march that would take us off camp for a bit of a traipse around the local kampongs and a general amble around the countryside. All very pleasant and we didn't even have to carry weapons or back packs. I guessed it wasn't a very serious route march because we turned back into camp after about three miles!

Far more dangerous was a hockey match arranged by someone who obviously didn't know how lethal hockey sticks could be in the wrong hands. I'm not saying that giving them to a bunch of rock apes was putting them in the wrong hands but, judging by the number of people limping at the end of the game, I'd say it was quite possible that they could have been placed in safer hands!

Warrant Officer Frank Sylvester was still dishing out his own brand of humour, some of which came my way. He came in to my stores one day with three very large boxes stacked up in his arms.

"Got something for you, Taff," he grinned. "Seeing as you'll be the only bugger left when we've gone you might need these." I opened up one of the boxes and found out that he'd given me the squadron's entire allotment of condoms!

There was a momentous farewell party over on Penang that left several comatose bodies stretched out all over the island and that was about it. I reluctantly handed my SMG back and all my webbing. No need for that where I was going. Jock went back to main stores and all that was left was to wish the lads well with a handshake before they all went their various ways. It's difficult to explain the effect my time with the RAF Regiment had on my life but I remember it as the best posting I ever had during my time in the RAF. I don't think I ever really settled afterwards. I made one attempt to get back with the regiment when I applied for the post of supplier with their Number 2 (Parachute) Squadron on my return to the UK but I was turned down as I didn't have the necessary trade qualification.

The Regiment didn't get many favourable comments from the rest of the RAF and a lot of disparaging remarks were made about them both then and probably now, I'd imagine. Maybe some of this bias is justified but I can only speak for myself when I say that I found them a tremendous bunch of lads. A bit rough around the edges perhaps but that probably had something to do with them having to do all the bloody awful jobs that nobody else wanted. They worked long and punishing shifts at Butterworth, often having to spend all morning loading and unloading AH accumulators (used to power the guns and observation posts). These steel clad batteries weighed twice as much as car batteries and had to be transported by three tonners. It was, as one of the lads recently told me, "A bastard of a job in that heat!"

1 LAA was a close knit squadron and I felt privileged to be a part of it. I enjoyed the boisterous company and I felt enriched by all the activities I took part in. I was going to say I enjoyed all the activities I took part in but that would probably be stretching the truth a bit too far! I was taken on board and treated no differently than any of the gunners. I freely acknowledge that they covered my back on several occasions when I may have stumbled and gone down on one knee for a

short count but that was par for the course with the RAF Regiment.

Maybe this book will help to enlighten those who are all too willing to be critical of the regiment. These are usually those with little or no knowledge of life on a regiment squadron. Then again, maybe it won't alter decades of prejudice but I hope at least to have given them an insight into what it's like being a penguin attached to the Royal Air Force Regiment. I think perhaps Rudyard Kipling may have got it right...

'We aren't no thin red 'eroes, nor we aren't no blackguards too
But single men in barracks, most remarkable like you; an' if
sometimes our conduck isn't all your fancy paints; why, single men
in barracks don't grow into plaster saints'.

(From the poem 'Tommy,' by Rudyard Kipling)

ENDPIECE

It took a very long time to re-acquaint myself with the RAF Regiment. When I left the RAF I was a bit busy raising a family and earning a crust to take much notice of service associations or reunions of any kind and it all faded into the background. It was only when a letter arrived inviting me to a boy entrants reunion that I began to think back on my service days.

I joined a talk group with other ex boys and that's when the stories began. I found that most of mine concerned the regiment and, at one of the reunions I was presented with a cuddly monkey to recognise my status as a U/T (under training) rock ape or 'pebble monkey' as they put it. It sits on my desk to this day, with a regiment lapel badge displayed proudly on his chest!

Through George Gault's RAF Regiment website I made contact with several of the lads who served with me in Malaya and it brought all the memories back of times long gone. The idea of putting them all in a book came much later, after I'd spent some time editing a book written by one of my ex boy entrant mates. It fired me up to start writing again and I decided to give my time with the RAF Regiment an airing. It wasn't too difficult to find the subject as, unknown to me; the moderator of our chat group had saved all my many stories in a folder. It was then just a matter of linking them together, removing some of the embellishments and outright lies and setting them out in as truthful a manner as possible! I hope I've succeeded in producing an entertaining read and I apologise in advance for any inaccuracies. Fifty years does tend to wear the memory down a bit and sometimes we remember incidents a little differently than others may. I've tried to be as accurate as possible but if anyone feels sufficiently outraged to comment then all I can really say is go and complain to the RAF Regiment. If they're anything like they were when I was with them though, don't expect a polite reply!

Printed in Poland
by Amazon Fulfillment
Poland Sp. z o.o., Wrocław